Poems that Speak to Us

Selected Poems
of
Steve Kowit

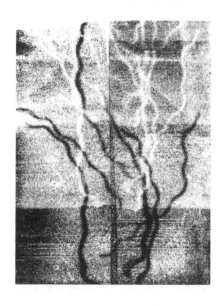

EDITED BY

JIM HORNSBY MORENO & JOSEPH D. MILOSCH

Garden Oak Press
Rainbow, California

Garden Oak Press
1953 Huffstatler St., Suite A
Rainbow, CA 92028
760 728-2088
gardenoakpress.com
gardenoakpress@gmail.com

First published by Garden Oak Press on May 1, 2021

ISBN-13:   *978-1-7350556-3-3*

Library of Congress Control Number: 2021935413

Printed in the United States of America

Steve, we dedicate this book to Mary and you. We honored her choices for this book and celebrate you and your gift of writing. We hope wherever you are now, you are smiling at our efforts.

In gratitude to Mary Kowit for allowing us to proceed with this project and with our abiding love for your help in its preparation.

— Jim & Joe

Contents

from *The Dumbbell Nebula* (2000)

from *The Gods of Rapture* (2006)

from *The First Noble Truth* (2007)

Poems that Speak to Us

Selected Poems
of
Steve Kowit

Edited by

Jim Hornsby Moreno & Joseph D. Milosch

End Papers by
Al Zolynas

Art by
Mary Kowit

GARDEN OAK PRESS

Reader, calm yourself: I am no agent of discord, no firebrand of sedition. I anticipate history by a few days.

— PIERRE JOSEPH PROUDHON
(from *The First Noble Truth*)

from

Lurid Confessions

A Vote for Harold

The kid who's taken the paper route for the summer,
a doughy, asthmatic schlemiel
with a blubbery bottom
& bifocals big as moondogs
& cockeyed hair
hasn't a shot at paperboy of the season
& two weeks in Miami.
For him a good day is passing the schoolyard
without getting punched in the head.
Our block is the worst. He has to pedal uphill
in the wind. You can hear him coming for miles,
straining & wheezing — then a forlorn
little squeal at the crest
like a possum shot from a tree
& a crash that rattles the dishes.
Then, after a silence, his broken,
woebegone voice among the azaleas.
I no longer lunge out of my chair like I used to,
but calmly stroll into the yard
& remove the handlebars from his thorax.
He blinks thickly, releasing a sob.
Together we salvage the home edition
that's scattered over the alley —
it too full of mayhem & ill luck:
an air disaster in Argentina,
a family of seven lost in a flood,
the hand of a refugee reaching thru barbed wire,
clutching at nothing, a hand so thin
it will eat anything — straw, dung, wind. . .
& then he is gone, wobbling into the gutter,
that exemplary herald of the Abyss
dogged on all sides
by curses & screeches & horns
& is lost in the distance
disheveled, & shaking his head
like a man who is forced to bear witness
to things too awful to mention,
& pedaling like hell.

Wanted — Sensuous Woman
Who Can Handle 12 Inches of Man

from an ad in the Miami Phoenix

She was sensuous to a fault
& perfectly willing
though somewhat taken aback.
In fact, at first,
she noticed no one at the door at all.
"Down here! . . . down here! . . ."
I shrieked.
— Need I add that once again
   I left unsatisfied.

The Creep

The creep moves in on strange women.
"Harold," he says.
"How ya doin' tonight?"

You clutch your purse.
Turn down what street you will,
he is beside you,

leaning in — the open lace
of an enormous sneaker
slapping against your ankle
like long, loose arms.

Lurid Confessions

One fine morning they move in for the pinch
& snap on the cuffs — just like that.
Turns out they've known all about you for years,
have a file the length of a paddy-wagon
with everything — tapes, prints, film. . .
the whole shmear. Don't ask me how but
they've managed to plug a mike into one of your molars
& know every felonious move & transgression
back to the very beginning, with ektachromes
of your least indiscretion & peccadillo.
Needless to say, you are thrilled,
tho sitting there in the docket
you bogart it, tough as an old tooth —
your jaw set, your sleeves rolled
& three days of stubble. . . Only,
when they play it back it looks different,
a life common & loathsome as gum stuck to a chair.
Tedious hours of you picking your nose,
scratching, eating, clipping your toenails. . .
Alone, you look stupid; in public, your rapier
wit is slimy & limp as an old bandaid.
They have thousands of pictures of people around you
stifling yawns. As for sex — a bit
of pathetic groping among the unlovely & luckless:
a dance with everyone making steamy love in the dark
& you alone in a corner eating a pretzel.
You leap to your feet protesting
that's not how it was, they have it all wrong.
But nobody hears you. The bailiff
is snoring, the judge is cleaning his teeth,
the jurors are all wearing glasses with eyes painted open.
The flies have folded their wings & stopped buzzing.
in the end, after huge doses of coffee,
the jury is polled. One after another
they manage to rise to their feet
like narcoleptics in August, sealing your fate:
Innocent. . . innocent. . . innocent. . . Right down the line.
You are carried out screaming.

The Rose

Home late, I eat dinner
& read the paper
without noticing
the rose in the yellow
glass on the dining room table —
not until
Mary shows it to me.
"Isn't it lovely?"
"Where'd you get it?"
"A fellow named Bill."
"Oh?"
"Just some guy who comes in
to the bar occasionally. . .
Isn't it lovely?"
"He gave it to you?"
I turn to the editorial page.
"Yes. . .
he just got out of the hospital."
She bends
& takes in its fragrance.
She is wearing that black negligee.
"The hospital?"
She straightens up & looks at me & sighs.
"He's dying of cancer."
We stare at each other.
I want to embrace her,
tell her how much I love her,
how much I have always loved her.
But I don't.
I just sit there.
When she walks back into the bedroom
I see it at last,
glowing on the table,
leaning toward me
on its heartbroken stem.

Joy to the Fishes

I hiked out to the end of Sunset Cliffs
& climbed the breakwater,
sneakers strung over my shoulder
& a small collection of zen
poems in my fist.
A minnow
that had sloshed out of someone's baitbucket,
& that I came within an inch of stepping on,
convulsed in agony.
Delighted to assist,
I tossed it back into its ocean:
swirling eddies sucked about the rocks,
white pythagorean sailboats
in the middle distance.
Kids raced the surf,
a labrador brought down a frisbee,
& the sun sank pendulously
over the Pacific shelf.
I shivered & descended,
slipping the unopened book
into my pocket
& walked south
along the southern California coastline —
all the hills of Ocean Beach
glowing
in the rouged light
of midwinter sunset.
Even now
it pleases me to think
that somewhere
in the western coastal waters off America
that minnow is still swimming.

405

I figured to leave early,
drive the coast road,
score a Chinese restaurant
& lay out by the ocean
for a while
& get stoned & write
& watch the women,
hit the buyers,
spend the afternoon with Bill,
catch the sun
sinking over the Pacific,
& be home for dinner.
But it didn't pan out:
I got off to a late start,
killed an hour in a bookstore,
settled for a jack-in-the-box
bean burrito.
The beach was out,
the buyers weren't in,
the sun went down without me.
Bill & I embraced
& parted
in a single gesture.
Around midnight,
driving back on 405,
it came to me
how quickly
everything was passing,
& suddenly
it was all luminous —
the abacus of lights,
the moon, cold
wind whipping
thru the window
& myself alive,
impermanent. . .
for the eleven millionth time
I vowed to change my life.

A mist came up,
the night settled in about me
& I dreamed sweetly
of all that I will never become —
women, wisdom, poetry & revolution
disappearing
in the purr of the engine
& the moan of the road
& the song of the radio.

Home

You arrive in Paradise feverish with anticipation, assuring yourself that everything will be perfect — no migraine headaches, no ambulance sirens, no goodbyes. & it's true, the view from your sitting room is breathtaking, the service impeccable, the food enticingly garnished, & although the water tastes slightly metallic, there is always the coke machine in the lobby. & the climate — the sort of weather you love, one glorious day on the heels of another. You stroll down the beach, under the mangroves & seagrape trees in love, as you were on Earth, with the word *oceano*, white seagulls, the bronzed & half naked women — women who are everything you have always dreamed, & yours for the taking. Truly a lecher's heaven. Yes, everything's perfect, perfect by definition. . .'til one afternoon in an unguarded mood you confess to yourself that the cuisine is without flavor & the wine flat, that the celestial muzak piped into your suite, however mellifluous, jangles your nerves. How you wish you could turn on the radio & hear Monk or Dylan or even the six o'clock news. You long, if the truth be known, for a cup of cold water. As for the women, however lovely to look at, to the touch they are as lifeless as the pages of the magazines from which they were drawn & as weightless & predictable as the figments of your own imagination.

It is just then — at that very instant — that the thread of a name & face catches the light on what remains of the delicate film of your cortex, the wraith of a memory. . .& escapes. You call to it desperately over & over, but it will not return, though its residue lingers on your tongue. Such is the other side of God's marvelous amnesia. From that day forward you are lost. You pace in distraction along the Elysian beach obsessed with the need to recall who it was & what it must have been like. How insufferable, at such moments, is the glare of Paradise! & so it is that with only your foolish heart as witness, you begin to long bitterly for home.

The Dead Magician

They surround me on the beach as well they should.
I am the drowned man, now worthy of what I suffered,
awesomely still, surrounded by approval
& terror. Eternal now, but for me
the sky could not be this blue,
nor the lone, low, predatory buzzard
gliding above the sea,
so black,
so deliberately beautiful.
Years later they'll recall a day in summer
when the whole of reality trembled like the white
sheet they covered me with,
thinking to mute my power.
A shoe full of small change,
a wallet & watch under a towel
wrapped in a shirt up the beach —

such was my life, such are the attributes
I have been emptied of.

The usual things. Dying
was one of the few occasions
that shook me out of my slumber.

They hauled me ashore — in death
a hideous fishlike creature,

much the sort that will surface up in one's dreams:
the head of a mythological beast —
grotesque, inhumanly bloated,
but almost familiar —
bobbing up out of the deep & then being sucked under.

Out of McHenry

Broken fence thru the mist.
Bitter fruit of the wild pear
& vines full of berries.
The stone path
buried in brambles
& mud
& the shack in ruins,
rotted thru
like an old crate:
half the roof caved in.
The whole place
gone to weed & debris.
Someone before me
sick of his life
must have figured this
was as far away as he'd get
& nailed it up
out in the void
then died here
or left
decades ago.
A swallow
skitters among the beams
& flies out
thru the open frame of a window.
Now nothing inhabits the place
but tin cans
covered with webs,
a mattress,
a handful of tools
busted & useless —
& myself
where he stood
here in the doorway,
in mist,
high up over this world.
Trees & flowers dripping with cold rain.

from

Passionate Journey

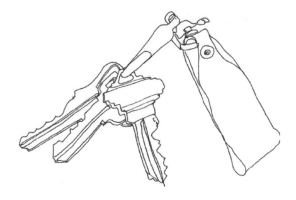

What chord did she pluck in my soul
that girl with the golden necklace
& ivory breasts
whose body ignited the river:
she who rose like the moon
from her bathing &
brushed back the ebony hair
that fell to her waist
& walked off
into the twilight dark —
O my soul,
what chord did she pluck
that I am still trembling?

— after Chandidas

When the water lily opens
in the fresh spring
it has not her charm.
Nor has the white moonlight
spilling over the hills.
When she moves
she sways
like a field of grain
in a summer breeze
but with more grace.
Even the peacock
is not as lovely as she.

— after the Tamil

Catching an unexpected peek
of the polished slope
of her lovely breasts
the young man
seems as astonished
as if he had suddenly
discovered himself
on a sheer ledge
high in the Himalayas
from which,
he can see at once,
he will never escape.

— after Panini

When he pressed his lips to my mouth
the knot fell open of itself.
When he pressed them to my throat
the dress slipped to my feet.
So much I know — but
when his lips touched my breast
everything, I swear,
down to his very name,
became so much confused
that I am still,
dear friends,
unable to recount
(as much as I would care to)
what delights
were next bestowed upon me
& by whom.

— *after Vikatanitamba*

Joyful is he who tastes his bride's red mouth
in a thatched pavilion screened against the storm.
Her moans & quickened breathing
that are mingled with the drops
that beat all night against the pumpkin vine,
& violent thunderclaps,
& moorhens
crying out against the driving rains.

        — *after Subhariga*

The city is sheer delight
with its markets
& highways
& elegant restaurants
& theaters
& parks
& the women —
the women
every bit as fetching
as everyone said
they would be.
& the climate perfect —
absolutely ideal!
Only sometimes,
at night,
walking along the beach
over the twisted roots
of the mangroves,
the ocean
calls me back
to that girl
with the dark eyes,
& those summer nights
we lay by the raging river
wrapped in each other's arms —
then I walk back
into a city
of nothing but shrillness
& gaudy illusion.

— *after Vidyapati*

Darling, I anticipated your arrival
with the first rains
but the river is at flood,
the storm is unrelenting,
the sky,
at every crack of thunder,
lights up with a lurid glare,
& still you have not come.
Once again I have sat beside your desk
all evening,
folding & unfolding your letter,
staring out the window at the dark.
Drunk with delight
all the frogs & waterbirds
are shrieking
& the peacocks dance.
I long for you.
My sorrow is unending.

— *after Vidyapati*

If you must go
then I won't stop you, but stay for an hour more, or half
an hour or
just a few minutes longer
at least
let me look at you, touch you. . .
do not run off before I have even gotten to know who you were.
Your voice is so lovely . . . let me feel what it's
like to rock in your arms one last time. Alive, we are two small cups of
water running into the sand. Who knows
if we'll ever see each other
again.

— *after Amaru*

Does that girl who used to gather hibiscus
at dusk, by the river,
recall our nights of abandoned love
in the reeds
& know that my heart is still hers,
or do only the screaming parrots remember?

— after Kapilar

Even now
I crush in my arms
like a madman
that girl with
vermilion lips
& lush breasts.
I ravish her mouth
like a parched root
drinking the rain.

— *after Bilhana*

Summer days, decades
ago, I would lie
by your side in
the shade of the willow
tree that was here
on the riverbank. One
day I would have
carved our names
on its bark
with a small knife
had you not said
no, do not harm it.
That day we swore
to love each other forever.
Uprooted,
that tree has been gone
many years. Now
you too are no more.
Today I stroll on the bank
by the thrashing waters
here where it stood
recalling your voice
& the beauty
& gentle grace
of your spirit — this river
that rushes
headlong into the sea. . ..

— after the Sanskrit

from

The Maverick Poets

Hell

I died & went to Hell & it was nothing like L.A.
The air all shimmering & blue. No windows
busted, gutted walk-ups, muggings, rapes.
No drooling hoodlums hulking in the doorways.
Hell isn't anything like Ethiopia or Bangladesh or Bogota:
Beggars are unheard of. No one's starving. Nobody
lies moaning in the streets. Nor is it Dachau
with its ovens, Troy in flames, some slaughterhouse
where screaming animals, hung upside down, are bled & skinned.
No plague-infested Avignon or post-annihilation Hiroshima.
Quite the contrary: in Hell everybody's health is fine
forever, & the weather is superb — eternal spring.
The countryside all wildflowers & the cities
hum with commerce: cargo ships bring all the latest
in appliances, home entertainment, foreign culture, silks.
Folks fall in love, have children. There is sex
& romance for the asking. In a word, the place is perfect.
Only, unlike heaven, where when it rains
the people are content to let it rain,
in Hell they live like we do — endlessly complaining.
Nothing as it is is ever right. The astroturf
a nuisance, neighbors' kids too noisy, traffic
nothing but a headache. If the patio were just
a little larger, or the sun-roof on the Winnebago worked.
If only we had darker eyes or softer skin or longer legs,
lived elsewhere, plied a different trade, were slender,
sexy, wealthy, younger, famous, loved, athletic.
Friend, I swear to you as one who has returned
if only to bear witness: no satanic furies
beat their kited wings. No bats shriek overhead.
There are no flames. No vats of boiling oil
wait to greet us in that doleful kingdom.
Nothing of the sort. The gentleman who'll ferry you across
is all solicitude & courtesy. The river black but calm.
The crossing less eventful than one might have guessed.
Though no doubt you will think it's far too windy on the water.
That the glare is awful. That you're tired, hungry, ill
at ease, or that, if nothing else, the quiet is unnerving,
that you need a drink, a cigarette, a cup of coffee.

They Are Looking for Che Guevara

The lecturer writes the phrase *free enterprise*
                         on the board in green chalk.
Above it white pustular fissures appear, which is the strangler
fig taking root in that part of the map devoted to Indonesia.
The metallic pit of the fruit grown from the miracle seed
                            of the green revolution begins ticking.
The peasants dig in. The secret bombing begins.
The porpoise & bison & whooping crane lie down
                      on top of the lecturer's desk & begin disappearing.
Meanwhile the Huns push on to the Yalu River
searching for Che Guevara.
The CIA is hunting for him in the Bolivian Andes.
Ferdinand Marcos & 6,000 Green Berets are hunting for him
                             in the Philippines.
Ian Smith is hunting him down in Zimbabwe.
A small flame appears in the map of Asia:
it is that part they have burnt down searching for Che Guevara,
                          queen-bee of the revolution.
They are hunting for him in Angola, Korea, Guatemala, the Congo,
                     Brazil, Iran, Greece, Lebanon, Chile.
9,000 Ozymandian paratroops drop over Santo Domingo
                     with searchlights, searching for him.
He is not there. He is gone. He is hiding among the Seminoles.
He throws the knife into the treaty with Osceola.
He conspires with Denmark Vesey.
In Port-au-Prince he is with Toussaint.
He reappears later at Harper's Ferry.
He is in Nicaragua, in Cuba where they have embargoed the rain.
The CIA has traced him to Berkeley, but he is in Algeria too
& Uruguay, Spain, Portugal, Guam, Puerto Rico.
Not all the ears of the dead of Asia will lead them to him.

He goes home, embraces his wife, embraces Hildita,
                        embraces the children of Buenos Aires,
gives his compadre Fidel an *abrazo*, lights his pipe,
pours a cup of *maté*, takes a pill for his asthma,
cleans his rifle, reloads it, writes the First Declaration of Havana.
Torpedoes of Intergalactic Capital, Inc. blow up
                        the screaming hair of the global village.
B52s drone overhead. It is dawn. They are checking every frontier.
They are looking for Che Guevara.

Notice

This evening, the sturdy Levis
I wore every day for over a year
& which seemed to the end
in perfect condition,
suddenly tore.
How or why I don't know,
but there it was: a big rip at the crotch.
A month ago my friend Nick
walked off a racquetball court,
showered,
got into his street clothes,
& halfway home collapsed & died.
Take heed you who read this
& drop to your knees now & again
like the poet Christopher Smart
& kiss the earth & be joyful
& make much of your time
& be kindly to everyone,
even to those who do not deserve it.
For although you may not believe
it will happen,
you too will one day be gone.
I, whose Levis ripped at the crotch
for no reason,
assure you that such is the case.
Pass it on.

from

Mysteries of the Body

Josephine's Garden

First thing in the morning the phone rings.
It's Mary to tell me that Jack,
who's been dying of AIDS for two years,
is finally gone.
An hour later the ophthalmologist
puts some sort of drops in my eyes
& for the rest of the day
the light is blinding.
When I go outside I have to wear
those dark paper shades the nurse gave me.
Even the pulpy gray stones
& the faded hedge & the pale green
spikes of the barrel cactus
in Josephine's garden
are too bright to look at,
while her roses & bougainvillea
blaze out as if someone
had suddenly flung back the shutters — as
blinding as one of those high-mountain blizzards,
but more gorgeous & painful.
If this is the way the world really is
it's too much to look at.
No one could ever survive it.
Nevertheless, all afternoon,
I keep stepping out into that garden,
eyes smarting as if someone
had rinsed them in acid,
astonished again
at the unbelievable colors,
the utter profusion of forms,
the sharp edges everything has in this world.

Perognathus Fallax

When I went to the shed to check for water
damage after the last rains,
I found a tiny gray mouse
dead among the stacks of old cartons,
& lifting out the rags & jars,
found his mate, backed in a corner,
tiny & alive. Beside her — ears
barely visible flecks, tails nothing
but tendrils of gray thread — two nurslings:
one curled asleep by her snout,
the other awake at her nipple;
the three together no larger, I'd guess,
than the height of my thumb.
I took the box into the yard,
where there was more light,
& where the cats weren't lurking,
& lifted out the rest of the detritus —
a shredded pillow, cans of varnish
& spray paint — beneath which I found, woven
out of what must have been pieces of cotton,
chewed cardboard & small twigs,
some sort of ramshackle nest.
With nowhere to hide, she scurried
behind it, a pup still at her dugs,
& looked up at me, into my eyes,
the way one of my cats might
who'd been cornered, or as might
one of my own kind, pleading —
her gaze wholly human, wholly intelligible.
It's uncanny, isn't it, how much alike we all are?
The next morning, when I went to the pump house
where I'd set the carton for safety,
I was amazed to see
the stunning filigreed globe
into which she had rewoven that nest, overnight:
from a small port at its top, her little snout
with those two bright eyes,
peering anxiously into my face.

I just stood there. I could hardly believe
how exquisite that nest was,
& how happy I was to see her.
The crumbs of seed I had dropped in
were gone, & I thought how good it would be
to keep them there, safe from the hawks,
feed them whatever they liked — but
for only a moment, then took out my knife
& sliced a small escape hatch in the cardboard,
an inch or so from the bottom,
& the next time I went back they were gone.
I was sorry to see the thing empty.
Is that stupid of me? *Perognathus*
fallax: the San Diego pocket mouse,
according to my *Audubon Guide*
to North American Mammals —
which was the last week of March,
the whole yard given over to mountain lilac
& sage & alyssum, & out by the wood
fence, that stand of iris,
too tattered, I'd thought, to survive
all those hard rains, but which had.
& under my feet, alive,
but so tiny one hardly noticed,
a hundred species of wild flower:
saffron & white & pink & mauve & blood red.

For My Neighbor's Daughter

Afraid that your eyes will smart
painfully in the summer's glare,
you seldom go out anymore
without those dark glasses.
Nor do you wear those fetching
summer dresses,
the ones that spin about
as you swirl down the street.
Is it because of this insufferable heat
that you have begun neglecting
your wardrobe & makeup,
& letting your long hair spill uncombed
down your back — this heat,
which has turned everything too bright,
too melancholic?
It is easier, I know, to find delicate
crystal that will not break
than a boy who means what he says.
Still, that is no reason
to sit in the dark
of your mother's porch,
night after hot August night,
with only the light of that small radio
glowing beside you.
Given a town filled with young men
who love dancing & fast cars,
do not, sweet child,
redden your eyes all summer long
for a boy who is not coming back.

Rain

When we were good
& done again
she slid the towel down
between her legs
stroking herself dry,
then sat up lazily
to pour another glass
of beaujolais
from the decanter
by the stereo.
From where I lay
I watched the notched
spine of her back,
her hair, which earlier,
when she had taken
out the pins,
had fallen
in such lovely
disarray
against her shoulders.
When she curled back down,
we lay there
for a long while
listening
to the slush
of tires
on the street —
the rain
that beat against the rocks
out in the courtyard
& was dripping
down the eaves. "It's
perfect, isn't it?"
she whispered,
snuggling up
against me. "Just
what we've been
needing all this time —
a good
hard
all-day rain."

Solo Monk

One day back in the '60s
Monk was sitting at the piano,
Charlie Mingus pulling at his coat
how Monk should put the word in
so the Mingus group
could play The Five Spot,
seeing as how Monk's already legendary gig
down there was ending —
                Mingus,
all persuasion & cajolery,
ran it down for twenty minutes
till he capped it with the comment:
    "Dig it, Thelonious,
        you know we Black Brothers
  GOT to stick together!"
At which point, Monk,
laconic to a fault
(till then he hadn't said a word), turned
slowly with a sidewise glance
& raised one eyebrow:
        "Ma-aan,"
     he said,
"I thought you was Chi-nese!"

                   & evenings, between sets,
Monk would pace outside The Five Spot,
head cocked to some inner keyboard.
With that listing gait of his,
that wispy black goatee,
that rumpled herringbone tweed hat
he sported in those days,
he'd pace that corner, solitary
        & quixotic
              in a rapture
    of exploding chords —
        all angular
  & dissonant
        & oddly phrased.

One summer night a Checker Cab
pulled up as he was so engaged,

                                        & Monk,

who happened to be passing at that moment,
swung back the door,
then stepped so quietly
& self-effacingly behind it
that you would have thought it was his calling —
but his ear as ever cocked
            to that imaginary keyboard.
                        An elegant patrician couple, clubbing,
— blond Westchester money —
stepped out on 8th Street like an ad for Chivas Regal.
                As the primped fox
sashayed past him in her saffron strapless,
tossing back her golden mane,
her escort nodded vaguely
not so much as glancing up
at that solicitous, albeit altogether funky
looking colored doorman
                    with the goofy hat.
A gesture almost too indifferent to be haughty.
& with that they hurried past & disappeared
into The Five Spot,
having come to hear the legendary Monk,
that droll & idiosyncratic piano.
        The sensation, Whitney Balliett wrote,
        of missing
the bottom step in the dark.

                            "— Eerie, isn't it,

            to hear him playing
                tho he's dead,"
Mary said,
playing Monk
the night we heard
he had died.

continued

& she lowered the dust cover
over the turntable
as quietly as Monk had shut the door
of that Checker Cab
& turning without sign or gesture
had gone off
bopping down the street,
head cocked as ever to one side
& circled by the halo
of that rumpled hat:
   oblivious. . .
     preoccupied. . .
       lost
in the sweet jazz of the night —
     Monk
   on 8th Street
  at the end of summer
in the early '60s.
   Must have been around 11:55.

Golden Delicious

When old Frieda Holden, the lady from whom
I would buy those wonderful apples, started raving
about the new young pastor
at First Church of Christ, Savior,
on Lansing & Mission,
I thought Jesus, I'm in for it now,
& tuned out — that is to say,
as I stood in the doorway
watching her bag two dozen Golden Delicious
out of a barrel-sized crate,
I nodded & grinned.
"Well that's awfully nice. . ." I would mumble.
You know how it goes — that catechism
of slavish politeness. Like one of those shriveled
colonial apple head dolls, the old lady
was nothing but wrinkles,
with blotched, cadaverous arms,
& hands that would never stop shaking.
Wasted away like she was she was scary
to look at. Now I've never liked Jesus talk much:
it jangles my nerves.
Nor do I have any great love for that merciless,
apoplectic Old Testament God —
a paranoid schizoaffective
fixated on vengeance. *No, frankly,*
I haven't the least bit of interest in either
your church or its priesthood,
is what I was seething to tell her.
Not, I suppose, as I'd like to believe,
from some urge to correct her view of the world
or deepen the level of discourse between us.
But simply to rag her. . .
that old instinct of mine
for schoolboy defiance: a braggart's need
to assert that I'd thought about things
more deeply than she had, was worldly
in ways that she wasn't, moved
in a universe larger by far

continued

43

than that circumscribed province of fruit trees
& churches & country politeness.

                              "Compassion,"
she said out of nowhere — or rather

half whispered.
"Isn't that now the root from which spirit springs. . ."
& handing over the bag
with the two-dozen apples,
she looked at me sweetly.
                              Had I been dreaming?
I stood there a moment embarrassed, fumbling
for change, then thanked her profusely
& stumbled back to my Datsun.

Halfway home, one hand on the wheel,
the other holding one of those juicy Golden Delicious up
to my mouth,
it hit me. Of course.
It wasn't an admonition brought on by something she'd seen, in some
creepy way, in my soul,
but merely a phrase that her minister used
that had stuck, & that she was repeating to me
in a context I'd missed.
And once that was clear,
the hard pit of breath caught in my chest
                              released itself from my throat, half
sigh & half laugh. In truth, nothing at all
had in fact passed between us but neighborly tidings.
                              The old convivial graces.
She'd simply been trying to give me some sense
of the man she so much admired,
& of the faith they belonged to,
& of who she herself was — the adamant spirit
under that crumbling flesh.
For all of my rage at her church, not a cell of me
wished the old woman less than good health & long life.
Or, since long life she had in abundance,
if there was anything to it, life everlasting.

& that settled between myself & my demons,
I took one more bite of that wonderful apple
& rose back into this vivid world.
In the last flush of daylight the roofs
of occasional houses & barns
caught the crimson of sunset. Horses & cows
stood about in their perfect stillness.
Behind them, this world, growing darker
— all ruddy & golden— had started dissolving.
                              Compassion —
isn't that now the root from which spirit springs,
rolled around on my tongue
with its fine, sweet taste,
till that too vanished
into the hum of the tires
spinning over that backcountry road
like some kind of music.

The Workout

Decked out in purple shorts & spandex tights
& party-colored jogging suits,
the votaries of fitness
have been trying to shape up.
While dervishes of Monday evening
high-impact aerobics
leap & jerk like frenzied zealots
in convulsive seizure,
& those dumbbell lifters grunting
into full-length mirrors
spend their workouts flirting
with themselves —
with their own sweet pumped-up repetitions
other flagellants have strapped their limbs
to squat-&-flex devices, chest expanders,
hip & thigh racks,
& are climbing dutifully the gravitronic
exer-stairway up toward skinny heaven.
Not unlike the penitents of other sects,
they are convinced that decades of decay
can be undone, & that the more one genuflects
the less one rots
that has got the aged, the adipose
& the misshapen
pedaling their stationary bikes
in such unholy fury
you would think they were outracing Time,
that hag who has been waiting at the finish line
to snip the thread,
& will not be outrun.
While every now & then
some sleek young thing in leotards
parades her killer body
to remind the women what they do not look like,
& the men, what they are not about to have
the pleasures of,
however long they bicycle in place.

A carnival of dreams is all it is
this imbecilic adoration of the golden calf
& bulging chest & tapered thigh,
this robigalia of compulsive nitwits & deluded
fools is just what I am thinking,
when I spot him riding toward me in that mirror,
flushed & puffing: my unpleasant-looking
older cousin with that stupid grin —
as smug & supercilious as ever: haggard,
baggy-eyed & self-impressed, his drooping middle
thicker than I'd ever have supposed.
Humiliated, frankly, to be seen with him,
especially in such a place as this,
I turn my gaze discreetly elsewhere,
for God knows we never have had
all that much in common —
I being by a long shot younger,
more athletic, slender, muscular & better looking.

A Pact

You won't forget either, ever, I know it,
that afternoon at Bittern Springs Lake,
years back, when you were twelve
or thirteen, & I managed to pull you
out of the water barely in time —
the two of us clutching each other
& trembling. "Honey, it's alright,"
I whispered over & over.
Later, still shaky but calmer,
we strolled thru fields of orangey marigolds
toward the motel where your mother
sat waiting for us
by a fountain of flickering lights,
the watermelon-red Sandia mountains
behind her, incandescent in the dusk.
How poised & womanly you seemed
as you hugged her, careful
to say nothing, knowing
it would have been pointlessly cruel. How
fine of you at that age to have seen that.
So neither one of us told her,
not then or ever, but all these years
it has been our secret.
That evening, the three of us sat
on the motel veranda — your mother,
radiant in a blue summer skirt,
myself jotting notes for a poem
that would never get written,
while you, whose young life
had all but been taken,
sat watching, astonished,
as you brushed your long hair,
a couple of high school kids
necking passionately in the shadows — your
whole being awakened, suddenly, I think,
for the first time,
to the mysteries of the body.

from

The Dumbbell Nebula

Worms   Mary Kawst

Beetles

The famous British Biologist J.B.S. Haldane, when asked by a church man…to state his conception of God, said: "He is inordinately fond of beetles."
— PRIMO LEVI

Spotted blister beetles. Sacred scarabs.
Water beetles whirling on the surface of still ponds.
Little polkadotted ladybugs
favored by the Virgin Mary & beloved of children.
Those angelic fireflies sparkling in the summer evenings.
Carrion beetles sniffing out the dead.
June bugs banging into screens.
Click beetles. Tumblebugs. Opossum beetles. Whirligigs
& long-horned rhino beetles.
Cowpea weevils snuggling into beans.
The diving beetle wintering in mud.
Macrodactylus subspinosus: the rose chafer
feasting upon rose petals, dear to the poet Guido Gozzano.
The reddish-brown *Calathus gregarious*.
Iridescent golden brown-haired beetles.
Beetles living in sea wrack, dry wood, loose gravel.
Clown beetles. Pill beetles.
Infinitesimal beetles nesting in the spore tubes of fungi.
There is no climate in which the beetle does not exist,
no ecological niche the beetle does not inhabit,
no organic matter, living, dead, or decomposed
that has not its enthusiast among the beetles,
of whom, it has been estimated, one and one-half
million species currently exist,
which is to say one mortal creature
out of five's a beetle — little armored tank
who has been rolling through the fields her ball of dung
these past three hundred million years: clumsy
but industrious, powerful yet meek,
the lowly, dutiful, & unassuming beetle —
she of whom, among all earth-born creatures, God is fondest.

Ronnie

Shortly after they'd scrambled his brain with electroshock,
I bumped into him on a Brooklyn street.
He had put on some weight, seemed calmer, less jangled.
No longer the manic young poet who'd bounce
about on the balls of his feet, barely touching
the street as he floated above it —
he had tricked back that garland of black curls,
sported, of all things, a jacket & tie,
& seemed, for once, at home in his body — grounded
the way the rest of us are, by the world's weight.
                              "Steve, I feel great!"
though his voice, too quick & emphatic,
made me uneasy: "A million times better off!"
And he opened his fist in a little explosion of fingers & thumb,
by way of dismissing, as if it hadn't really been his,
that earlier life:
                    "Though sometimes. . .I. . .
I guess I forget things. . . ." & with that
it collapsed: the sanguine, implacable mask electro-
convulsive shock had made of his face
crumbled along the line of his mouth, & his eyes went hazy.
He looked scared, like a man who wakes up
& doesn't know where he is, his own name, what city
he's in, or whose body: that old,
impetuous storm squelched to a kind of stolid confusion.
              The northeast heaves,
                  O loveliest of winds to me —
a line from one of his exquisite Hölderlin versions
swam through my head. The street glistened with rain.
Leaves spun at our feet. We made the sort of talk
people make. Shook hands: "Ronnie,
it's great to see you again!" Only an awkward civility
kept me from hugging him, weeping — & then hurried off,
though thirty years later, having heard he was gone,
I set the phone to its cradle & stood
in the dark, wrenched back to that street
& to all that had never got said, & that telling you of
has taken me back to again — the sorrow
& love I had left there, unspoken between us:
his fitful, disquieted spirit; the poem of his life whirling about in my head
— a tumult of leaves in a gust of uneasy wind.

51

Crossing the Desert

Finally I got up & walked over to the couple at the next
fire ring. "Look," I said quietly, "I'm trying to sleep."
"Pal," the guy looked up, "this here is our
campsite & we'll talk as long as we goddam feel like."
He had on a blue Padres cap & was sprawled out
in the tent on his belly, with a six-pack of Coors,
& she was outside on a folding chair by the fishing rods,
swinging a leg that was marble in the moonlight.
The last thing I needed was trouble, but I took a step
toward him anyhow. "It's midnight," I said, hunkering down.
"I don't think you have any idea how —"
"Buddy," he raised himself on one elbow, "I'll tell you this
one last fucking time —" But I turned around & walked off.
In the dark, among strangers, you never know
what can happen. He must have thought I was going back
for a pipe-wrench, or my .22, because there wasn't
a sound after that. I dragged my mummy bag
out of the tent & as I lay there in the stillness,
circled by the silhouettes of camper shells
& Winnebagos, everything grew suddenly strange — as if,
unmoored from time, I'd stumbled on the ruins
of some ancient caravan. A savage & nomadic people
is how they'll remember us a thousand years from now
when we're not even dust anymore, is what I was thinking,
lying there under those billion stars, the silence broken
only by the thin, electric buzz of the cicadas, wind
rasping in the chaparral, & what must have been
the canopy of someone's tent out in the darkness, flapping.

Refugees, Late Summer Night

Woke with a start, the dogs barking out by the fence,
yard flooded with light. Groped my way to the window.
Out on the road a dozen quick figures
hugging the shadows: bundles slung at their shoulders
& water jugs at their hips. You could hear,
under the rattle of wind, as they passed,
the crunch of sneakers on gravel. *Pollos,* illegals
who'd managed to slip past the Border Patrol,
its Broncos & choppers endlessly circling
the canyons & hills between here & Tecate.
Out there, in the dark, they could have been
anyone: refugees from Rwanda, slaves pushing north.
Palestinians, Gypsies, Armenians, Jews. . . .
The lights of Tijuana, that yellow haze to the west,
could have been Melos, Cracow, Quang Ngai. . . .
I watched from the window till they were lost
in the shadows. Our motion light turned itself off.
The dogs gave a last, perfunctory bark
& loped back to the house: those dry, rocky hills
& the wild sage at the edge of the canyon
vanishing too. Then stared out at nothing.
No sound anymore but my own breath,
& the papery click of the wind in the leaves
of that parched eucalyptus: a rattle of bones;
chimes in a doorway; history riffling its pages.

Madly Singing in the Mountains

Fred Moramarco & I had been hiking
up in the Cuyamacas,
lost in our usual babble, boring
more holes in the world than the woodpeckers do:
talking the angels out of their halos,
the muses out of their tutus,
the world into marshmallow pudding.
From post-deconstructionist theory
& newfangledness in poetics,
we'd moved on to Salvadoran death squads
& low-intensity warfare;
the legions of evangelical zealots out on the streets
agitating for more executions,
compulsory prayer, ironclad regulations
against miscegenation & condoms —
a jihad against homosexual teachers,
the ACLU, & *The Bob Dylan Songbook*.
They wanted fellatio outlawed,
the braceros deported,
the fossil records revoked.
The trail we'd been hiking had swung northwest
thru stands of black oak,
till suddenly it opened onto a ridge
& we stepped thru a tunnel of branches
into broad daylight.
The sky impossibly blue.
East — mountains that rolled on forever;
west — where the light was hazier still,
the mesa dissolving into a mist
we supposed was the coast. Fred
thought he could almost make out the ocean,
though at that distance, in that light,
whatever was out there had faded
into the gray Pacific wash of the void:
one of those moments when,
stunned by the infinite, everything stops.

"Jesus," Fred sighed, "I'm glad
we got out here today."
& I nodded "Yeah, me too, me too!"
& before we even knew we had been there,
were back into Jimmy Swaggart
& Schrodinger's Cat;
the friendship of Po Chu-i & Yuan Chen;
those child prodigies: Mozart, Arthur Rimbaud
& Traci Lords; no-fault divorce;
every-moment awareness; *Muji* — the first gate;
the marriage of Chaos & Form;
& the hypothetical origins of carbon-based life.
In such manner making our way
to where Green Valley Falls
tumbles into the Sweetwater River Canyon.
We too merrily babbling away — tongues
like party-streamers in high wind.
Delighted. Oblivious. Full steam ahead.

Jacumba

       I am sitting in the restaurant of the spiffy
new air-conditioned Jacumba Motel
& Health Spa, sipping a root beer
& staring out at a desert
so blazingly desiccated & stark
it's hard to imagine that anything
other than lizards & buckthorn survives here,
& wondering where the old Jacumba Hotel
disappeared to,
that rambling, stucco monstrosity
where one summer night we....
Well, what's the use. Without that hotel
this town is nothing at all of the crumbling,
moth-infested ghost-town it was,
blistering out in the Anza Borrego,
halfway to Yuma,
exquisitely shabby & brooding.
Ah, Time — with your ferocious improvements!
Your infernal, confounded meddling!

I Attend a Poetry Reading

The fellow reading poetry at us wouldn't stop.
Nothing would dissuade him:
not the stifling heat; the smoky walls
with their illuminated clocks;
our host, who shifted anxiously
from foot to foot.
Polite applause had stiffened
to an icy silence:
no one clapped
or nodded.
No one sighed.
Surely he must understand that we had families
waiting for us, jobs
we had to get to in the morning.
That chair was murdering my back.
The cappuccino
tasted unaccountably of uric acid.
Lurid bullfight posters flickered
in the red fluorescent light —
& suddenly I knew that I had died,
& for those much too windy readings of my own
had been condemned
to sit forever in this damned cafe.
A squadron of enormous flies
buzzed around the cup of piss
I had been drinking from.
Up at the mike, our poet of the evening
grinned,
& flicked his tail,
& kept on reading.

A Whitman Portrait

You know that portrait of him that caused such a ruckus?
The one where he's propped in a cane-back chair
striking a pose so grave & heroic
you'd swear at first glance it was Odin or Lear
or — Ah, but at that very moment you'll notice,
as just about everyone finally does,
the butterfly perched on his right index finger.
& then you can see that Walt's sitting there
under that rakish sombrero & beard, grandly amused,
as much as to say: How splendid it is to see you, my dear,
& what a propitious moment to call. . .
You can guess how his critics stewed over that one!
They'd fling up their arms in maniacal fury
& swear up & down that the thing was a fraud.
Why it's nothing but papier maché! they would shriek.
A cardboard & wire photographer's prop!
Which slander, however absurd & transparent,
the populace simply assumed to be fact —
'til just last September when high-resolution spectro-
analysis proved what any fool could have guessed:
she was just what she seemed, mortal & breathing,
a carbon-molecular creature like us: *Papilio*
aristodemus, now all but extinct;
the very swallowtail, golden-banded & blue-tipped,
that archeo-lepidopterists claim
could have been seen all over Camden that summer:
one of the millions scooting about thru the woods
& fields around Timber Creek Pond. Only, for whatever
odd reason, this one had taken a fancy to Walt.
When she wasn't flitting about in the fennel & parsley,
the neighbors would see her light on his wrist
or swing thru his beard or perch on his shoulder
like some sort of angel, or sprite, or familiar.
How he did it we don't know exactly,
but as the photographer set up his camera
Walt sat himself down by the open window
& hummed a few bars of Donizetti's La Favorita,
at which simple tune that bright little beauty
flitted in from the garden as if she'd been called to.

If it's true there exist fake butterflies
cut out of paper & wire, my guess is
they belong to a later generation of poets.

In any case, this one was made of the same stuff
as we are — felt pleasure & pain in abundance:
lit first on the broad brim of his hat, next
at his knee & at last on his finger. Was greeted by Walt
with a gruff, friendly laugh as one of his cronies —
at which precise instant the chap with the camera
(he could hardly believe his remarkable luck)
pulled down the lever that triggered the shutter —
preserving forever that singular flight
of felicitous whimsy — this portrait at once majestic
& tender & bathed in affection & grace & delight:
Walt Whitman & butterfly. Camden, New Jersey. 1883.

The Blue Dress

When I grab Big Eddie, the gopher drops from his teeth,
& bolts for the closet, vanishing
into a clutter of shoes & valises & vacuum attachments
& endless crates of miscellaneous rubbish.
Grumbling & cursing, carton by carton,
I lug everything out:
that mountain of hopeless detritus — until,
with no place to hide, he breaks
for the other side of the room, & I have him at last,
trapped in a corner, tiny & trembling.
I lower the plastic freezer bowl over his head &

Boom! —

slam the thing down.

"Got him!" I yell out,

slipping a folder under the edge for a lid.
But when I open the front door, it's teeming,
a rain so fierce it drives me back into the house,
& before I can wriggle into my sneakers,
Mary, impatient, has grabbed the contraption
out of my hands & run off into the yard with it, barefoot.
She's wearing that blue house dress.
I know just where she's headed: that big
mossy boulder down by the oleanders
across from the shed,
& I know what she'll do when she gets there — hunker
down, slip off the folder,
let the thing slide to the ground
while she speaks to it softly, whispers
encouraging, comforting things.
Only after the gopher takes a few tentative steps,
dazed, not comprehending how he got back
to his own world, then tries to run off,
will she know how he's fared: if he's wounded,
or stunned, or okay — depraved ravisher
of our gladiolus & roses, but neighbor & kin nonetheless.
Big Eddie meows at my feet while I stand
by the window over the sink, watching
her run back thru the rain,
full of good news. Triumphant. Laughing. Wind
lashing the trees. It's hard to fathom
how gorgeous she looks, running like that
through the storm: that blue

sheath of a dress aglow in the smoky haze —
that luminous blue dress pasted by rain to her hips.
I stand at the window, grinning, amazed
at my own undeserved luck —
at a life that I still, when I think of it, hardly believe.

from

The Gods of Rapture

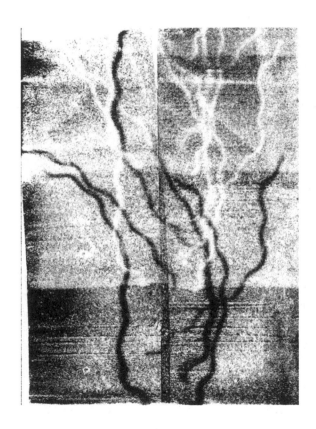

Others saw him too
as he stood at the edge
of the ripening field
asking for work.
          He
who held a canvas satchel
over his shoulder came,
he said, from the land
where the summer west wind
makes flute music
out of the little holes
that the bees bore
in the swaying bamboo
& the cold water falling
over the rocks
is the music of drums
& monkeys shriek
when a peacock
dances about
on one of the hills
like a young woman.
          Friend,
is it possible
I am the only one of all
those who saw him that day
who tosses about in bed,
night after night,
with a grief
nothing has caused,
& arms clutching the darkness?

                    — *after the Tamil*

Where the swollen Monongahela
washes the Alleghenies,
wind perfumes the air with fine pollen
& butterflies flicker among the vines
& birds
abandoning all modesty
sing of paradise
in the cool branches.
Here young girls
whirl about on the hillside,
their summer dresses
billowing out
like colorful petals.
Soon, young men will join them
& they will shriek with delight
& chase each other & dance
& couple
by couple vanish
into the swaying field
where honeybees feast
on the bells
of delicate flowers.

— after the Sanskrit

Do not speak to me of that irresistible flute
at whose plaintive & passionate note
the devoted housewife
slips from her couch,
drawn like a thirsty doe to the stream,
& the mendicant sage
who dreamed he'd forsaken
the world of illusory forms
strays from the True Path.
Seduced by that haunting air
even the aged & infirm
make fools of themselves.
Friend, if even the tiniest creatures
dance rapturously
when they hear that promiscuous flute,
what chance does an innocent
girl such as I — already
more than half mad with desire —
have to resist?

— *after Chandidas*

Though she enjoys
slipping her lips
to my mouth
when no one is looking
& doesn't object
to my hand
fondling her breast,
she is still like a child
who loves to ride
around in a toy cart
& gallop about on a horse
whose tail
is a piece of rope
nailed to a broom
handle, & has not yet
got the idea
of the pleasure
of mounting something
faster moving than that
& life sized.

— *after Tumpicerktran*

If she denies it she is lying —
there were witnesses:
two purple gallinules
among the spatterdock;
a heron,
standing motionless
on one long
reed-like leg;
& silver minnows
leaping
in the moondrenched waters.

— *after Kapilar*

Because she has been running thru a summer downpour
& arrives at the young man's apartment all
disheveled, breathless, rain
drops dripping from her dark hair, her
sandals drenched, her sheer
blue sundress wringing wet
& clinging to her,
is it any wonder
after only one embrace,
solicitous of his beloved's welfare,
the young man quickly helps her out of her wet things?

— *after Yogesvara*

It was brutal. A country boy
without an iota of skill
in the art of love-making,
he scratched up my back,
manhandled my breasts,
bit on my throat,
& when he finally entered,
his boyish strength
was too much for me.
He was immense —
savage —
insatiable!
I pleaded & cried out,
but in vain.
I swear,
had the vow
not been sealed with a kiss
I would never meet him
again tonight
as I promised I would.
But it was,
& I cannot go back on my word —
it is out of the question.
I would run over thorns
with my bare feet
to be there on time —
for with me,
as you well know,
honor comes first!

— *after Vidyapati*

Her loveliness defies description.
No god bloated with dyspeptic
righteousness
could have created her.
More likely
she's the daughter of the Moon
with its seductive
& incantatory light,
or of some woodland sprite,
or of the warm spring rain —
she who is,
among all creatures of this world,
the most ravishing.

                        — *after Kalidāsa*

In the madness
of the white light
of the moon
near high reeds
where croaking frogs,
beating like drums,
frightened
a small bird
from the field,
I trembled
& he swore
he would not leave me.

— after the Tamil

Dusk,
in the wake
of my grief
over him
to whom
I have given
my heart,
do not
torment me.
Only
the cruelest
of hunters
would
take aim
at a terrified
doe
caught
in a flood
& struggling
for life.

— *after the Tamil*

At last, in
a harsh, almost
inaudible whisper
the foreigner
spoke
of the wife
he had left behind.
Then
his voice broke
with a moan
so piteous even
now when the story
is told the
quarrels
of lovers cease
& householders
shake
their heads & business-
men consider
postponing their
travels abroad.

— *after Amaru*

As a young woman she had been admired
by any number of boys most of whom
she thought rather stupid & coarse.
Then a young man she much liked
seduced & betrayed her, & another treated
her poorly, & one disappointment led
to the next till she gave up on the whole
sorry business & kept her distance from men.
Embittered & chastened, she taught school
there in that village for thirty-four years.
She had two or three dear friends & a sister
whom she loved, & that sister's four
children whom she adored & would shower
with gifts. & thus did she age there
where others mated & wed & gave birth.
Now & then, on beautiful summer days,
she would stroll by herself through the fields
to a marvelous pond in the woods not far
from the spot where her parents were buried
& the house where she had been raised,
& would sit there at the pond's edge
watching the noble dragonflies
scurry about & bright, silvery fish just under
the surface, how they would scoot here
& there, & she'd smile & relish her life &
give thanks for this beautiful & mysterious world.

— after the Tamil

Unable to bear
the sight
of her last
staggering steps
& raising
his great head,
the mate
of the wounded elephant
bellows at heaven
again & again
shaking the forest,
the whole world
with his grief.

— *after the Tamil*

from

The First Noble Truth

Snapshot

At night, a man is sitting at his desk in pain, aging,
full of fears & dreams, till Jesse barges in
& nuzzles his left leg & says, Hey,
you know that open box of milk bones
in the kitchen? Well, I've been thinking…
The man washes down another vicodin,
scratches the dog's head, & the two of them
get up & leave the room. When he returns,
he sees how dark it is outside, & late.
He types & stops, looking for a phrase he can't
quite find, some gesture that the past
had given him & taken back.
Above his desk, that ancient snapshot of his folks,
two Lower East Side kids, their lives together
just beginning, who will never understand
that everything the future holds for them
has passed. Dexter Gordon's hushed
& melancholic take on "Don't Explain" drifts
quietly across the room, as if that saxophone
knew, somehow, that the fellow staring
at that photo had been weeping, stupidly
& over nothing. At the keyboard, Sonny Clark
looks over once at Dex & nods, & shuts
his eyes, & listens to himself — to both of them.
Staring out the window at the dark,
the man finds, he thinks, at last,
what he's been looking for, & goes on typing.

That Dog

we saw behind the hospital when I got out,
all agitated, racing back and forth along the fence,
clumps of hair pulled out in ugly patches,
had been waiting — now of course I understand
it — to be dragged off to some basement lab
where they would strap him to a table
& then slice his tongue out of his mouth,
or snip the cerebellum from its stem,
or set him flaming like a torch
in one of those burn research protocols
the NIH delights to grant.
He wagged his tail at us, & through the chain-link
tried to lick my hand. Kneeling
outside the fence, I said: *Hey, buddy,
how's it going?* — assured him everything
was perfectly okay, & then walked on.
We hardly knew each other then.
Twice, you had been kind enough to visit me.
Up there, on Buena Vista Hill, crossing Parnassus,
I took your hand for the first time: the two of us
already half in love, & pleased, as lovers are,
with everything: the heart unwavering,
the day spun out of light, our human
brethren trustworthy & good. Ourselves
enraptured & oblivious,
unconscionably innocent & young.

The First Noble Truth

World Lit 241: Not surprisingly, they love *Siddhartha.* But when
I pick up the chalk & write on the board DUKKHA: THE FIRST
NOBLE TRUTH: SUFFERING PERMEATES LIFE,
no one looks pleased. After a moment of general grumbling
Marie Elena mumbles out loud *I'm not sure that's true,*
at which Deegan pipes in *it's pure bullshit*! & that breaks
the ice & everyone laughs, but a laugh like an undercurrent
of angry disdain buzzing the way damaged wires back in the wall
buzz when they're ready to blow out the lights. Then Carlos
Padilla leaps to his feet & says *suffering — Hell, that's just
the tiniest fragment! Life is joy to the max! Just walking around
in bare feet or drinking a cold Fanta, or sitting around eating lunch
with a couple of homies, or sweating bullets out on
the basketball court*: ripped, feisty, full of exuberant health, Carlos
defending our common lot with such good-natured,
passionate faith even I can't help but grin, cheering him on.
When he's done with that funny harangue half a dozen
start clapping — But there are some who remain unconvinced,
for whom such a notion does not seem such a betrayal,
a blasphemous, incomprehensible lie. A few of the older ones
in the back of the room, & Sean & Ty & Ahmad for sure —
While the ones filled with the optimistic, undauntable juices of life
are clapping & laughing, those few sit quietly at their seats,
their faces darker, more inward. One stares at the back
of his hand. Another listens politely, stroking her long, gray
beautiful hair, — those who, I gather, well understand that
the world is weighted with sorrow. Dukkha, the First Noble Truth.

The Burro

That little plaster donkey we broke down & bought
at that ramshackle roadside souvenir shop
years ago, while waiting at the Tijuana-San Ysidro
border crossing was, but for the dark umber
they had painted her, a perfect likeness of those
burros climbing thru the mistbound mountains
of Chiapas, bundles of firewood strapped
to their backs & their slender necks & heads bowed
slightly in the harness: uneasy servants
of the people who had built Copan, carved Palenque,
plotted the ecliptic for a thousand years, centuries
before the pious Spanish Christians came
to swing them from the trees & steal their land...
Whole families of Indians from Tenejapa
& San Juan Chamula — even the 10- & 12-year-olds —
hunched under bundles of *leña* & *carbon*. When
a family would tap timorously at the door of our adobe
house in San Cristobal, I'd say yes, of course,
& they would ease the tumplines from their brows
& slide those heavy bundles from their backs,
& then unload the patient, small, dust-colored burro
who'd be standing by them in the courtyard,
silent & resigned. Half the night those people
had been trudging down those rocky mountain
trails, barefoot, in their threadbare black *chamaras*:
husbands, wives, kids. . . & we would pay
for all that wood & charcoal with a few
measly pesos & a handful of tortillas. With a crack,
like the lash of a whip, that little plaster burro
shattered one spring morning of her own weight,
chalky shards beneath the picture window where she'd
stood — who silently, for years, had been
a keepsake to us of that other life — long-suffering
servant of the long-suffering servants of the Mexican
sierra: that little plaster burro at the window
in the light, by the African violets & the wandering Jew.

Personality Parade

After Watergate, wasn't Richard Nixon secretly committed to a mental institution run by Quakers and replaced by the CIA with a Hollywood double? Isn't this the real reason why his wife, Pat, refuses all interviews because she is afraid reporters will ask about the look-alike she is living with, and she will have to tell?

— M.P., New Brighton, MN.
(Walter Scott's Personality Parade)

When they carted Dick off that morning,
Pat was frankly upset. It wasn't just
that they'd caught him making his
I-am-innocent speech out on Park Avenue,
naked except for his black inaugural tie,
or because of the screams of that little girl
they'd found in the basement, tied to a drainpipe —
after all, Dick had done crazier things in the White House.
But it was dread of another scandal,
one more call from the Washington Post,
another smug chuckle from Walter Cronkite.
She was sick & tired of wearing dark glasses,
a fake rubber nose & a thick mustache in public.
So when Central Intelligence mentioned
a permanent rest-home for Dick in Tierra del Fuego,
Pat jumped at the chance, though at first
when the Hollywood double showed up at the door
she'd had her misgivings. A failed vaudevillian,
he could never pass thru the dining salon
without leaping up on the table
for one final chorus of *Sweet Georgia Brown,*
his glazed eyes rolling like Eddie Cantor.
He'd softshoe his way thru their afternoon strolls,
break into Gene Kelly routines when no one
was looking, tell unfunny jokes from the '30s.
His squirt-in-the-eye boutonniere never amused her.
He reeked of a dozen colognes.
It was only at night, on the springs,
that she had to admit that his flashy showbiz routines
were a hundred percent more entertaining
than Dick ever was with his shrill little whines
& pasty caresses & minuscule twanger.

When she thought of the old days
she'd let out a heartrending sigh — of relief,
& bending down as he jawed on the phone with his agent
or checked thru the casting calls in the latest issue
of *Billboard,* she'd offer her sweet little hoofer a peck
on the cheek — at which he would drop whatever it was
he'd been doing, & grinning, give a little flick of his head
so the bowler he wore indoors & out would slide down
his arm in a deft double-gainer & land at his fingers —
Pat's cue to two-step around him, & taking his arm
they would *pas-de-deux* into the bedroom
popping their heads out once thru the doorway
by way of finale, the whole number accomplished,
if you can believe it, while belting out a novelty
two-part arrangement of *Blue Skies. . .*
      nothing but blue skies from now on.

Memorial Day

Because our sons adore their plastic missile launchers,
electronic space bazookas, neutron death-ray guns,
a decade down the pike it won't prove difficult
to trick them out in combat boots
& camouflage fatigues,
rouse them with a frenzy of parades, the heady
rhetoric of country, camaraderie & God.
the drum & bugle & the sudden
thunder of the cannon as they march
into Hell singing.
Which is the order of things.
Obedient to a fault, the people will do as they are told.
However dispirited by grief at the graves
of their fallen, the mother returns at last to her loom,
the father to his lathe,
& the inconsolable widow home to raise sons
ardent for the next imperial bloodbath:
                    Ilium. Thermopylae. Verdun. Pork Chop Hill.

For Chile

In the offices
of Anaconda-
Kennecott
cigar ash
drops
into an ashtray
like a severed head.

In the streets
of Santiago
the long struggle
of Lautaro
& Manuel Rodriguez
goes on,
as the heaviness
of a man's heart
becomes the heaviness
of his fist.

Invocation to My Muses

Never having had a muse to call my own, I bought
one of those dollar-ninety-eight cent novelty ballpoint pens
in San Francisco with a pair of winsome if diminutive
young bathing beauties in the barrel's
laminated plastic window, & adopted them.
Now when I spew forth my homicidal odes against the Pax
Americana, maledictions at the banks & the shenanigans
of finance capital, philippics on the snuffing of entire populations,
strophes full of *weltschmertz* & angst,
my laminated muses in their little string bikinis
are a constant source of solace & of inspiration.
& when I pen paeonics to the Absolute,
that ballpoint bounding like some Chassid Master
or Mavlavi dervish dancing on the rooftops in a rapture
of transcendent union, my two voluptuary muses run
playfully among the dunes of every cursive.
Wallow as I will in the most metaphysical & speculative slough:
my choriambics on the noumenal & the mysterion,
hendecasyllables upon continual creation,
Anselm's Argument & Rodney Collins' catalogue of the invisible,
they hang on every word: they do not flit about
from bard to bard & bed to bed like fickler muses
but are modest, steadfast, chaste & loyal.
Whatever be my measure or my mode: be I apostrophizing,
rhapsodizing, waxing lyrical or wringing dry the tissue
of the heart, or simply sketching dithyrambic
jubilees to the quotidian, poetry in praise of almost anything,
my fetching midinettes remain as decorous as Lady Astor,
steadfast as Penelope, as faithful & as innocent as honest labor,
fuzzy mittens, chamomile tea. . . Or so they seem
when that sleek pen-point figure-eights along the page.
But — O wretched moment — when the inspiration flags
& my elbow leans against the armrest so that my pen,
upended, points skyward like a suppliant toward Heaven,
& my mini-terpsichoreans, perforce upended, upside-down,
are standing on their heads like fallen women,
then things grow sticky!
For obedient in that posture to some cosmic law known only
to our Beloved Maker, those little sky-blue two-piece swimsuits
clinging to their saucy torsos start unaccountably dissolving!

It's miraculous! Astonishing! Unnerving!
My muses start a slow, seductive, disconcerting & mysterious
disrobing! — some newfangled kind of gravity-induced
striptease that renders them as naked as a pair of peeled tomatoes,
nude as two pre-apple Eves, or as Susanna ogled in her garden
by the Elders, or as Artemis the day Actaeon went to pieces
having seen her in the altogether, bathing — irresistibly, libidinously,
shamelessly & absolutely naked! naked from their flowing
tresses to their tiny painted toenails! O my own sweet Thalia & Erato!
Dear uninhibited half-sisters, nude from minuscule erectile areolas
to those furry little swollen mounds of Venus — O music never
to be finished! Porlockian aborted visions! *Poetastus interruptus!*
Jettisoned illuminations! Epiphanies adrift upon the swift,
amnesiatic waters of the void! & yet, withal, blithe spirits,
I do swear, despite the fact that my interminable apostrophes
upon your nubile, sweet & lickerish anatomies
continually distract me from completing my sublime librettos
to the Infinite, my Orphic hymns to the Millennium, & even
if it comes to that, forever blows my chance to cop a Prix de Rome,
MacArthur Prize or Guggenheim, I will — I swear —
prove equal to your inspiration — I will rise to the occasion.
I will not forsake you, ever! But prove worthy
of those much maligned though everywhere obliquely honored,
warm, priapic, & exalted pleasures of the flesh!
O lasciviest of muses, for your own parts, when I roll your tiny
midriffs through my fingers, like a stricken, inarticulate King Kong,
facing for your lusty sakes the murderous concerted armies
of the critics — prove ye likewise faithful!
May your uninhibited striptease inspire verse forever fecund,
vibrant, earthy, gracious, steadfast, wise & strong!
      Sweet dames, runne softly till I end my song.

Eurydice

Everything you've heard about that irresistibly
seductive lyre of his is true.
& yes, the birds would light upon the overhanging
branches & grow still
to hear him pluck its strings.
No creature who had ears would not be moved —
& it was not alone that music, but himself,
that he was sweet & passionate & innocent,
that won me to him. As with everything
about that boy, his love
was absolute. Exquisite music
not because his hands were lithe
but that his spirit sang — though truth to tell
he was in many ways a child: impetuous, unthinking,
willful in the way a child is, who
in his singlemindedness
& the immensity of his desire
cares nothing that the matter is impossible.
Am I to blame him for that one mistake?
Is one to blame the child who overturns
the lamp & sets the house aflame?
No, no! He loved me. I will not betray —
It was his nature — foolish. . .well, perhaps,
but how cast blame? Who else, inflamed
by such enraptured grief would have stormed Hell
to lead me back into the sun-drenched earth?
We climbed through this abysmal dark for days,
myself so close behind
I could have stretched my hand & touched
his shoulder blade, if touching were a thing
the dead could do. — Oh, who would be so cruel
that she would blame that boy whose only crime
was childish impatience & impulsive love
— whose only fault was that he longed for me
so fervently that when he saw at last the rosy
light of that bright world above the hills
that mark the cusp of Hell,
his overwhelming joy was such he could not help
but turn — that boy whose willful, rash,
uncomprehending face, however beautiful,

I dare not call back fully to my heart
lest everything that I am loath to feel
be felt, & my composure burst; that face
which, from the very start must have possessed
that fatal, childishly oblivious last glance,
that whirled me back into this bitter dark.

The Bridge

Climbed up past the ridge,
slipped off my pack,
& sat there
on that viewy overhang,
the emerald vista
vast & luminous
as I'd remembered.
A pair of hawks
circled slowly far below.
The world is opulent,
indifferent, undeceitful.
Still & all, its latter purposes
elude us.
Brushing away a fly
that had been buzzing
at my skull,
I dug out of my pack
a pippin apple.
At my feet, flakes of mica
glistened
in the faceted conglomerate,
& to my left, suspended
from two stalks
of mountain lilac
past their bloom,
a miniature bridge:
the swaying membrane
of a web
some solitary spider
had abandoned —
a single strand,
half glowing in the light,
& half invisible.

Night Falls in the Lagunas

Sun down. Clouds massed above my head.
I hike alone — distraught, disquieted.
Sliver of lightning like a hairline fracture,
But no rain.
Stellar jays squawking in the Jeffrey pines
thru which a bone white three-
quarter moon is rising.
Then the frenzied yapping
of coyotes in the dark. They too,
unreconciled to this world. Coyotes,
crying out to one another from all sides.

Rest Stop

Needing to piss, I pull into the rest stop off Interstate 10, halfway
between Tucson & Casa Grande. It's three in the morning.
The creosote-scented sage desert so delectably hot
I could weep for joy. Then too, there's that full orange moon,
almost too good to be true. Man's fate, when all's said & done,
isn't the issue. On the wall above the urinal someone
has written LIBERATE JESUS. Liberate Jesus? Outside,
some guy, asleep in the bed of his blue GM pickup,
is happily snoring. Three guys hunker by the stone fountain
smoking & shooting the bull. A handful of unlit rec v's. An elderly
woman, her husband checking the map, leans on her walker,
sucking the juice from a pear. Behind them, nothing but desert.
Palo verdes & yucca. Not a single subdivision or mall.
After we're gone — not just this infinitely sanctimonious nation-state,
but the whole duplicitous, bloodthirsty species — it will still be here.
Well pleased, I slide back into my little yellow Tercel,
& cruise onto 10 West. The couple, the guy catching some sleep,
the friends hunkering there in the night, smoking & chatting,
I wish them all well. As for Jesus, let him fend for himself.
I slip in another cassette. Figure to make Yuma by dawn.
I think of Jesus putting that curse on the Jews; Jesus flinging
millions of souls into Hell. The puffed-up, fantastic beliefs
of this tiny featherless biped. Those too, gone soon enough.
I take a deep breath. Delicious! Delicious! The night about
as fragrant & paradisical as it gets. Spectacular moon low
in the west. Ronu Majumdar's bamboo flute. Desert on both sides.

Kelly Park

Late fall: gray macadam Brooklyn afternoon.
The Brighton local rumbles on its trestle
over Kelly Park. My pals & I are riding
3-speed bikes around the baseball field,
the big kids belting fungoes toward the fence.
This bike of mine is blue & yellow
with a rusted bell
& does not have a right-hand rubber grip.
Half a century, & still
how cold that naked handlebar against my palm.
Right here I lean into the wind.
& here, at last, the wind is at my back.
Look! This is the moment when I pick up speed.
At the crack of the bat, the ball
at once both rises toward the left field fence
& drops into some fielder's waiting glove —
all this in one swift parabolic arc.
Who could have guessed
it would rush by so fast.
November. Brooklyn. 1950 something. Kelly Park.

The Grammar Lesson

for Dorianne

A noun's a thing. A verb's the thing it does.
An adjective is what describes the noun.
In "The can of beets is filled with purple fuzz,"

of and *with* are prepositions. *The*'s
an article, a *can*'s a noun.
A noun's a thing. A verb's the thing it does.

A can *can* roll — or not. What isn't was
or might be, *might* meaning not yet known.
"Our can of beets *is* filled with purple fuzz"

is present tense. While words like *our* and *us*
are pronouns — i.e., *it* is moldy, *they* are icky brown.
A noun's a thing; a verb's the thing it does.

Is is a helping verb. It helps because
filled isn't a full verb. *Can*'s what *our* owns
in "*Our* can of beets is filled with purple fuzz."

See? There's nothing to it. Just
memorize these simple rules. . .or write them down:
a noun's a thing; a verb's the thing it does.
The can of beets is filled with purple fuzz.

For the Ones Passing Through

Astonishing, isn't it — all of these odd-
looking creatures darting around
in the grass — the lizards
& spiders & foraging bugs,
& the ones that are nothing but specks
of color flitting around
on invisible wings,
each with its own private sorrows
& pleasure,
its one precious life.
How strange it is
to be here at all
talking to you like this
in a poem,
if just for a single brief instant —
two spirits momentarily touching.
Isn't it weird?
Don't you feel it too,
how unspeakably odd everything is?
Friend, walk mindfully here:
Cause no intentional harm.
Even the least of these creatures,
the most minuscule sentient speck,
longs to live out
its one brief season on Earth.

Denis, Some Photos

It's not the one of you on the steps with Andy & Robert & Phil,
the 4 of you mugging with macho cigars: four tough union scrappers,
or the one in the corduroy jacket & dark biker shades,
or the broodingly handsome young stud in the wool sweater,
scraggly of beard & your rock-star hair gorgeously long,
God knows who snapped it, more than a decade ago.
Or the one at the table, amused & relaxed next to Alma, who's beaming.
Not even that juicy portrait of you in your leather jacket & baseball cap
standing next to Norma Hernandez, looking so much yourself, so fully
alive that it's scary, so beguiling & scruffy, so filled with that vivid,
dashing, mischievous air you had always about you. Denis,
you're so close in that photo I think I could take one little step forward
& hug you again. But not even that one. The one that I'm talking about
is you by yourself in the desert, at sunset, in shadow. Maybe
it's east of Santee or out in the Anza Borrego. You in your jacket & jeans,
right arm extended behind you, palm open, gesturing back
toward those incandescent mauve hills, the sky a luminous blue
brushed with the purples of dusk; in the uppermost left a white cloud
fringed in sandia red like some kind of halo: ethereal, mysterious. You
in the quiet dark with that puckish grin: half Irish wit & half tender grace,
pleased with it all. The sweep of your arm as much as to say *Look!*
This is just what I meant. What I've been trying to say the whole time!
See, it's exactly this I've been wanting to tell you. & after it's snapped,
I can just hear that wry, ironic half-grunt of your satisfied, shy
metaphysical laugh. The one of you by yourself, in a gesture
of absolute welcome, under a sky glowing at sunset, behind you those hills
& that white oracular cloud far to your left with its rapturous halo, portent
of all things that cannot be spoken. & you, ever the sweet host. *C'mon,*
you're saying. *Let's keep on walking. We'll get even closer.* It's that one.

Denis Callahan 1957-2006

from

Cherish:
New and Selected Poems

A Prayer

If it wasn't for Mary who knows all too well my oblivious nature,
I'd never have noticed those tiny, crepuscular creatures
floating around in the dogs' water bowls. The big, fat yellow
jackets are easy enough to spot & easy to save — You just
cup your hand under their bellies tossing them free with a splash
& they'll stumble back to their feet like indignant drunks, shake
out their wings, & fly off. But I'd never noticed those minuscule
midges & gnats till Mary pointed them out. At a casual glance
they are nothing but dust motes & flecks of debris.
By the time I bend over to look, a few have already been
pulled under & are hopelessly gone. But the ones still floating,
the ones still barely alive but alive nonetheless, you can lift out
on the tip of your finger, then gingerly coax onto dry cardboard
or fencing or whatever is lying around — though for gods' sakes
be careful! A single slip can prove fatal. But If you're patient
& steady enough, you'll see wings delicate as the lash of a small
child's eye, at last start to flutter. What has been saved,
though easy enough to disparage, is somebody's preciously
irreplaceable life. Given this planet's unending grief, let us
save whom we can. Eons after the last hominid skull has
crumbled back into the loam, may swarms of these all
but invisible creatures' descendants coast still, at dusk,
over these hills. May they find water & food in abundance.
May every breeze upon which they sail prove benign.

Passing the Potrero Graveyard

It isn't often I see someone in that little country graveyard
on Potrero Valley Road, but this morning as I drove past,
two women, each clutching a bouquet of flowers, were walking
toward a polished granite headstone in that solemn
& deliberate way that people walk when visiting their dead.
An hour earlier you'd left for Minneapolis. Your folks,
in their mid-eighties now, are clearly failing. When you get in,
they'll fuss & laugh: perhaps the last time in this world you'll
ever see them. I think of that baronial Jewish cemetery back
in New Jersey where my parents are laid to rest. For a moment,
driving through the Barrett Hills, I long to be there, kneeling
where they lay, to kiss their graves &, weeping, tell them that I —
well, you know the stuff that people always say, as if the dead
were lying there awake & listening. Dearest, I already miss you.
For a week I'll try to stop complaining — though it's my nature —
& make do: I'll pour birdseed in the feeders for the finches
& grosbeaks & jays, remembering how vulnerable all of us are
& how briefly everything exists. I'll feed our furry little
sweethearts & make certain Wally has his final dose of Baytril
& take Jesse for his walks — that slow, difficult circle he makes
these days around our modest property — & hide his Tramadol
& Condroflex in glops of cream cheese, per your instructions,
& as I promised, every second day I'll water the tomatoes & the
jasmine & the bougainvillea & roses & ice plant & the crape myrtle.

A Note Concerning My Military Career

After I'd sent the army my letter of resignation, two beefy Intelligence types
showed up at my place in the Fillmore with a huge reel-to-reel tape recorder,
& without mincing words, I tore into America's despicable agenda:
the circle of hell reserved for the savage carpet-bombing campaign
against the people of Vietnam & the puppet state that the U.S. was trying
to force down their throats. Which was why, I explained, I wouldn't put
their fucking uniform on ever again & why, if I had to fight, it would be
for the other side.
       Quiet, courteous, polite, they sat there for two hours
listening to my ferocious rant till I asked what exactly it was they needed
to know, & one of them said they had really been sent to find out if I
was planning to shoot President Johnson, or do something else of that sort,
& I laughed & said no, & we shook hands & they packed up & left.
But a month later, when the army sent me the transcript to sign & return,
I brought it instead to a young San Francisco attorney whose family firm
did *pro bono* work for resisters, & Butch Hallinan read that whole eighteen-
page harangue & looked up & told me how much he liked what I'd said,
& when I asked him what to do next, he advised me to get the hell out of town
as fast as I could. Which I did. I ran for my life & for the lives of all those
they were trying to get me to kill, & of nothing I've done in this world
have I ever been prouder.
       Listen, if you're reading this poem & you're young
or desperate enough to think of enlisting, or have already been suckered in,
understand that despite all those self-righteous fairy-tales about freedom
& peace, this nation has been from its genocidal beginnings addicted
to empire, plunder & perpetual war. Those combat flicks you watched as a kid,
& the sanctimonious propaganda that passes for news, & the swaggering,
hawkish prattle puked from the lips of our politicians & pundits—that spew
stinking of corpses & money — are meant to convince young men
& women like you to massacre, city by city & village by village,
America's villain *du jour*, adding, every few years, another small state
that stepped out of line to its necklace of skulls.
& for those of you who will march to your own graves in so doing,
the powers that sent you will bow their heads & present to your folks
the flag that was draped on the box they carted you home in.
       Friend, find any way that you can to resist
or escape. If you have to run for your life, for chrissake, run for your life.

Three Gents

for Fred & Al

We've been strolling down the beach, three elder gents
discussing matters subtle & abstruse, as is our wont:
Occam's Razor, Zeno's paradox, the Nimzo-Indian Defense.

While twenty-somethings jog & swim, toss frisbees, crest
the breakers on their longboards, shmooze or flaunt
their pecs & abs & legs & lovely breasts, we gents

with roving eyes are parsing out the elements
of Rational Decision Theory, Pascal's Triangle, the daunt-
ing issue of the cubic & the Nimzo-Indian Defense.

O rapture of beguiling flesh! Whither? Whence?
The Prisoner's Dilemma, Drake's Equation, Hume or Kant:
That redhead in her string bikini thong. Three anadipsic gents

guzzling down Foucault, ontogeny, unknowable events,
antimatter, counterfactuals, the permutations of Necessity & Want,
these grains of sand, uncountable, the ontological significance

of Fibonacci numbers, breasting waves, time's sting, the dance
of Eros, chance, Pyrronian regress. Pierced by the point-
ed horns of this Body-Mind Dilemma. Lost, three elder gents,
in dreams, the carnal itch, the Nimzo-Indian Defense.

Progeria

Those kids who age prematurely:
at seven already sclerotic & grey.
& I too! Though at first glance
I seem a man long past his youth,
Just a day or two back I was a boy
tossing a softball out in the schoolyard.
This wretched, incurable curse!
One moment of sheer exuberant joy
& the next you're bent, deaf, gasping
for breath, your flesh splotched,
& hands that will never stop shaking.

from

Steve Kowit's Greatest Hits

Last Will

If I am ever
unlucky enough to die
(God forbid!)
I would like to be propped up
in my orange overstuffed chair
with my legs crossed
dressed in my favorite sweater & jeans
& embalmed
in a permanent glaze
like a donut
or Lenin
a small bronze plaque
on the door of my study
showing the dates
of my incarnation & death.
& leave the room as it was!
Let nothing be touched in the house!
My underpants stuck on the doorknob
just where I left them.
My dental floss
lying on top of the Bhagavad Gita
next to my socks.
Let the whole of Ebers Street
be roped off
& planted with yew trees
from Narragansett to Cape May
& left as a monument to my passing.
The street?
No — the city itself!
Henceforth
let it be known
as the Steve M. Kowit
Memorial Park & Museum.
Better yet
if the thing can be done
without too much fuss
put the whole planet to sleep.
Let the pigeons & buses
& lawyers & ladies
hanging out wash
freeze in their tracks.

Let the whole thing
be preserved under ice
just as it looked
when the last bit of drool
trickled over my chin.
Let the last of the galaxies
sizzle out
like a match in the wind
& the cosmic balloon
shrink down to a noodle
& screech to a halt.
Let time clot
like a pinprick of blood
& the great solar flame
flicker down
to the size of a *yertzite* candle
leaving the universe dark
but for one tiny spotlight
trained on the figure of me
propped in my chair —
for after my death
what possible reason could life
in any form
care to exist?
— Don't you see
it would be utterly pointless!
I would be gone!
Look, try to conceive it,
a world without *me*! Me
entirely absent —
nobody here with these eyes,
this name,
these teeth!
Nothing but vacant space
a dry sucking wind
where I walked
where I sat — where
you used to see me
you would see nothing at all —
I tell you
it dwarfs the imagination. . .

continued

Oh yes, one last thing:
the right leg
is to be crossed over the left
— I prefer it that way —
& poised on the knee.
Prop the left elbow up
on the arm of the chair
with a pen
in my right hand —
let my left
be characteristically
scratching my skull
or pulling my hair.
If you wish
close the lids of my eyes
but whatever you do
the mouth must remain open
just as it was in life —
yes
open forever!
On that I absolutely insist!

Lullaby

— *after Atila Josef*

Sweet love, everything
closes its eyes now to sleep.
The cat
      has stretched out
at the foot of your bed
& the little bug
      lays its head
in its arms
& your jacket
that's draped on the chair:
every button has fallen asleep,
even the poor torn cuff. . .
      & your flute
& your paper boat
& the candy bar
      snug in its wrapper.
Outside,
the evening is closing its eyes.
Even the hill to the dark
woods
has fallen asleep
on its side
      in a quilt of blue snow.

Other Favorites
and
Uncollected Poems

Taedong River Bridge

in memory of Jerry Greenberg

Retreating, Walker's 8th Army torched whatever lay in its path,
battered Pyongyang with rockets & mortars till the whole
besieged city crumbled in flame. Blew up the granaries, too,
& the bridges & roads, so that those who didn't freeze to death
would be sure to die of starvation — vengeance against the Chinese
Red Army & the peasant armies of North Korea for beating them
back to Inchon. The U.S. command shelling that city till nothing
remained but that one standing bridge: tangle of girders with hardly
a place to find footing & nothing to hold as it swayed in the sleet
of the wind over those waters — Taedong River Bridge, the only
way left, short of death, to cross out of Pyongyang. Ten
thousand terrified souls swarming over its splintered ribs.
On their backs, in their arms, whatever they owned or could carry.
Women cradled their infants. Men strapped what they could
to their shoulders. The crippled & dying & blind inching their way,
for to slip — & hundreds of those fleeing slipped — was to vanish
into the icy hell of that river. Then the others would clutch one another
& wail in that other language of theirs, while they kept moving.
What else could they do? For what it was worth, those
who fell through saved the lives of those inching behind them,
letting them know where not to step next.
                                                    Jerry,
that's what you did for me, too. Now & again, that awful black limo
pulls up at the curb in front of our house back in Flatbush,
& Henrietta, your mother, steps out, gaunt as death in that black
cotton shawl while I watch from an upstairs window. At which moment
my own beloved mother slips into the room, lays a hand on my shoulder,
& tells me, quietly, lest I say the wrong thing when her dearest friend
enter the house, what she had hoped never to
have to tell me at all: that you had been killed at the front.
I was twelve. Forty years later I remain stunned. Now & again,
something triggers it back & I drift out to Kelly Park
& watch you fast break down court — that long, floating jump
from the corner. The swish of the net.
                                                    Jerry, I don't know
you'd care,
but when my number came up for the next imperial bloodbath
I gave my draft board the finger — for us both. And for every last
terrified soul on both sides. I can't tell you how grieved I am still

that you're gone. Or thank you enough for the warning: your death
letting me know where I stand, who my real enemies are,
what the heavy money had in store for me too.
In a way, then, I owe you my life: more than anyone else, you
were the one who showed me where not to step next

— the one up ahead, in the bitter wind of the past, who fell through.

The Garden

Years ago we owned two cats who hated each other.
When I said we had better give one away
you wouldn't hear of it — you
were adamant, outraged. . .
relenting only weeks later when it was clear
they were going to tear each other to shreds.
I remember the speech you made:
if it came to that we would give away Sluggo,
our lovable calico,
who could purr his way into anyone's heart.
For in less tolerant hands, Mphahlele,
our difficult, misanthropic gray
might be abused, or abandoned. . .or worse — whereas
if he lived with us he would be loved always.
& of course you were right,
tho God knows you have paid dearly
for a compassion as absolute
& unyielding
as the copper sheet of the Mexican sky
rising each morning over that house
high in the hills of Chiapas
that you loved so
with its eleven rooms,
those great hanging bells of datura,
that courtyard, tangle
of wild vines
that you would never let me weed
to begin a garden,
insisting in that quiet way of yours
that every creature
had as much right to live as we had,
& that it was a garden.

Cutting Our Loses

In a downtown San Jose hotel;
exhausted & uptight & almost broke,
we blew 16 colones & got stewed on rum.
You lounged in bed
reading *Hermelinda Linda* comics
while I stumbled drunk around the room
complaining
& reciting poems out of an old anthology.
I read that Easter elegy of Yeats
which moved you,
bringing back that friend of yours
Bob Fishman, who was dead.
You wept. I felt terrible.
We killed the bottle, made a blithered
kind of love & fell asleep.
Out in the Costa Rican night
the weasels of the dark held a fiesta
celebrating our safe arrival in their city
& our sound sleep.
We found our Ford Econoline next
morning where we'd left it,
on a side street, but ripped
apart like a piñata,
like a tortured bird, wing
window busted in, a door
sprung open on its pins like an astonished beak.
Beloved, everything we lost — our old blues
tapes, the telephoto lens, the Mayan priest,
that ancient Royal Portable I loved,
awoke me to how tentative & delicate
& brief & precious it all is, & was
for that a sort of aphrodisiac — though bitter
to swallow. That evening
drunk on loss, I loved you
wildly, with a crazy passion, knowing
as I did, at last, the secret
of your quietly voluptuous heart — you
who have loved always with a desperation
born as much of sorrow as of lust,
being, I suppose, at once unluckier,
& that much wiser to begin with.

For the Kids

Against the lush green of the Allegheny woodlands
noisy schoolkids scramble down a makeshift stairway
of boulders to the muddy river.
I'd join them, but their teacher, a young,
well-meaning fellow,
holds me there with his chatter:
                "no fish anymore. . . .
the stripmining did it. . .
the sulfur. . ."
I shake my head with appropriate public dismay.
                the river,
its deep bed gives everything space,
lets everything breathe,
cuts a wide gorge thru the landscape
                  & triggers release.
It is May. Polluted or not the river
refreshes the senses. The spirit awakens.
The teacher's voice fades. Detached,
I am lulled from the every-dayness of things
                to their poignance.

The sun beats down on my head like a fatal drug.

The kids run about on the rocks at the water's edge.
The teacher talks on about dams
while the shrill voices of the kids
call me down to the river:
                "Steve. . . Steve," they sing out
hoping to thereby entice me onto the rocks.
One would whisper her secret; others wish me
to look at their unfinished poems,
or to spell this or that
& I scream down at them, hoarse,
with a stuffed nose,
                "Yes, okay, you can
put your feet in the water, but be careful —
don't mind the spelling. . ."
Crystal loses her sock. Another can't think
what to write. They clamber over the bank.
                "Put
the river in the poem," I shout.
But nobody's listening.

                                        "No. Not pollution. That's
not what I mean. Look. Look at the river. . . ."
My attention scatters like seed,
as if I hadn't the right to look at the river in peace.
& I haven't. I'm not being paid
to float off on my own.
Beneath me the brown, muddy Potomac gurgles over
the rocks & turns silver
in minuscule rapids & falls
& calls forth in us that which is changeless
& flows thru all things.
The river defies us, is ceaseless,
& will not hold still for our poems, & the poem's
unimportant, a pretext, & the kids know this,
or rather, they simply don't give a damn,
they don't need the poem,
but they jump over the rocks shouting & singing
& are one with the day, the mountains, the water.
They flow. They are artless. There is only this
festival gladness. There is no poem other than this,
no sifting of things, no discontent.
Life at this age is enough. If it weren't for us
they would surely strip out of their clothing,
out of their skins,
fling themselves into the river, swim off
where we couldn't hope to reach.
But we hold them back, we hold
them for our own good, our own ends. Even so,
see, they are barefoot out at the edge of the rocks
with their feet in the water.
                                    "Steve. . .
Steve. . ." they call out.
                                    & I come to them
running down to the river over the stones.

Intifada

Intifada

They only see one thing: we have come here and stolen their country.
Why should they accept that? They may perhaps forget in one or two
generations' time, but for the moment there is no chance.

— DAVID BEN-GURION
(quoted in *The Jewish Paradox* by NAHUM GOLDMANN)

Because Nebuchadnezzar, the Chaldean king, & his Babylonian armies
destroyed the First Temple, & the Court of Judah suffered expulsion,
and because of the sword of Merneptah,
the sting of the lash of Assyrian armies, & legions of pious Crusaders
condemning the Torah to flames, & we were led off by halters,
enslaved in Armenia, Georgia, the Caucasus,
                    because we suffered Chrysostom's rage,
Luther's Hitlerian frenzy, the Dominican fathers' Inquisitorial cross,
because we were numbered among the transgressors,
scattered among nations, expelled from the Rhineland, Bavaria, Spain,
brought as the lamb to the slaughter at Prague, Nemirov, Tarnapal, Bar,
Salonika, because we were dragged thru the streets of the *shtetl*
& set to the torch in the *shul*, were crucified, blinded,
                              boiled in oil & buried alive,
because we were stuffed into cattle cars & our neighbors said nothing,
were gassed in the showers, died screaming for mercy,
                              & no one protested,
am I now to rejoice that my Palestinian brothers & sisters,
dispossessed of all that was theirs by Ben Gurion's bloodthirsty
armies of conquest & plunder, are even today being chained at the wrist,
blindfolded, mocked, spat upon, kicked to the ground,
                              pummeled & bloodied
& left there to rot in the heat of the Negev?

Because the *Einsatsgruppen* mowed down the Jews in the streets
do I turn my back now and forget that the farmers of Khan Yunis
were murdered in cold blood, that the shepherds of Kafr Quasim
were shot where they stood, that the massacred women & children
of Dier Yassin were flung into wells, that the village
where Mahmoud Darwish was born no longer exists, that seven
hundred & fifty thousand indigenous Palestinian Arab people
                              were ethnically cleansed,
forced to flee for their lives to the squalor of refugee camps
while the sanctimonious Zionist settlers stole all that they owned.
That the infants & aged & sickly who could not survive that
tormented journey are buried out there where they fell.

118

Am I to forget that unspeakable terror, that despair?
Am I to forget that the Palestinian homeland was stolen?

My *mishbucha* look elsewhere, turn away with a thousand excuses.
Benny Morris & Ari Shavit shake their heads gravely: "Don't you see,
had we not done those unspeakable things, our wonderful Jewish
state could not have come to exist?" Amused, from their graves,
Joseph Goebbels & Philipp Bouhler wink at each other & grin.

Because of the curfews, expropriations, expulsions, the knock at the door,
because of the Anschluss, the *Kristalnacht* riots,
because of the boot of despair & the cheek of denial,
because we have suffered the smokestacks of Auschwitz,
the mass graves of Chelmno & Belsen,
because we fell at the walls of the ghetto,
am I to pretend now that the people of Ramla, Al-Lyd, Balad al-Shaykh,
Khisas & Haifa — those shepherds & farmers & teachers & merchants
& mothers & workers — have not the right to return to the land
that was stolen, the land that is incontestably theirs,
the land that their fathers had tilled for a thousand years.

Because I am Ashkenazi, a Jew, son of the tradesmen of Krakow,
Lithuanian fiddlers, Talmudic scholars, the wandering peddlers of Minsk,
child of the Khazar diaspora, exile — as are we all — in this world,
am I not of the Amalekite people as well, part Moabite, Chaldean, Toltec
& Pawnee, son of a long line of Canaanite cobblers, Nigerian ploughmen,
child of those who escaped here from Melos, Soweto, Sharpsville,
Zimbabwe, Belfast, Jakarta? I am Kurdish, Armenian,
of the wandering Romani people, of Calcutta's untouchable
Harijan masses, part Lacandon, Quiche & Yana, of Tasmanian blood,
born of the Sac-Fox nation, son of the Bayou, a runaway field slave,
sojourner, nomad, pariah, *untermensch*, heir to this world of nettles & dust.

That is to say, I am of the shebab, of pure Palestinian blood,
A Fedayeen son of Jerusalem shepherds, child of *al-Nakba*, son of those
with the bayonet at their throat, the ones beaten, raped, & expelled
by Ben-Gurion's terrorist settler militias.

continued

119

Should I forget the Lebanese dead? The blood of Shatilla & Sabra?
Am I to forget that Ashbir Yusef & Mahmoud Sabad were beaten to death,
that Sohel Zantut's son is still missing,
                                    that Fadhi Salim has lost his right leg,
that Sohel El-Ali was thrown from a bus, that Tamer Dasuki was shot
in the back, that Mustafa Hamden was buried alive, that the husbands
& sons disappear into prisons & the women weep by the rubble of stone
& cement that had once been their homes in the Gaza to which
they had fled, and yet manage somehow still to go on — what choice
do they have?—while the Gush Emunim & the minions of Valdman,
Schmuel Derlich, Zeevi, Begin, Shamir, Kehane, Sharon, & Bibi the Yahoo
parade thru the streets, cursing the filthy *Arabushim*. Am I to forget
the apartheid wall that steals yet more of the land & makes life
more unlivable yet, the Bedouin villages razed to the ground,
                                              the sociopathic
shelling, that slaughter of women & children huddled in school rooms
& shelters, & bekippad Sabras dance thru the Tel Aviv streets chanting
gleefully: *No school tomorrow in Gaza; all of their children are dead.*

While the villagers pray & the young men throw stones,
                                    I stand in the shadows
& watch. I say nothing. Shots have been fired. A handful of men
are hauled off for beatings & administrative detention:
Their confessions are written in Hebrew. A mother runs thru the darkness:
Mustafa, she whispers, Mustafa? . . . Mustafa?
                                    I hear the sharp breath intaken,
the all but inaudible weeping, the desperate vows of revenge. I note well
the names of the dead, whose homes the Occupation forces demolish,
the names of the children the settlers have kicked to the ground,
I note who is missing, whom the soldiers have beaten, whose land this time
has been taken. In the back seat of the taxi, Samia Mahmoud is trying
to breathe, a girl of 14 who will die if her father & she are not permitted
                                              to cross.
But the IDF soldier who stands at the checkpoint, a boy of 19,
looks at the papers her father's trembling fingers unfold & shakes his head
No:
                         They will not be permitted to cross.

Should I pretend I heard nothing? Saw nothing?
That none of this was my business?
Am I to forget that Israel Zenger declared that the Arabs must be removed,
& that Yosef Weitz & Chaim Weizmann did also?

& Ben-Gurion swore he saw nothing wrong with compulsory transfer,
& Golda Meir has vowed that now that they're gone
                                  we will not let them back?

About the scald of the rope of bondage pricking my throat I wrap
the kaffiyah. Let the young men take up their stones. Let the people arise.
Let the lamps of the priests of the Lord of Plunder sputter & darken.
Let the armies of occupation tremble. What was dread
has been sharpened to mettle & festered to gall. I will no longer
listen in silence. Do I too, like my Zionist countrymen,
                                  keep my mouth shut?
Do I simply say nothing? Just turn my back?
                        Do I too become the Good German?

Because of the *Oremus et pro perfidis judaeis,*
                        that terrible Good Friday Prayer,
Because of the teargas attacks & the nighttime raids & the endless arrests,
Because "Redeeming the Land" is a circumlocution for theft —
that never-ending settlement project,
I stand with this heavy stone in my hand: unbending, defiant.
Because of the Easter pogroms & the Nuremberg Laws
                        and the Aryan Clauses,
Because of those who have stood here before me
to say "This cannot be done in my name," I can no longer be silent,
because of *Gush Shalom* & the *Yesh G'vul*, & *Breaking the Silence*
& *Women in Black*, & because of the terrible fate
of *The White Rose*, I stand my ground at the edge
of an olive grove in the village of Dir Istya. I can do nothing
no longer. The theft of the Palestinian homeland tears at my soul.
By virtue of Military Order 938 & the uncodified
Jewish State Statute of 2014, in Occupied Palestine
the Palestinian flag is not allowed to be raised.
                  Here, in this poem, I raise the Palestinian flag.

Afterwords

A year ago, Jim Moreno approached me with the idea of compiling a posthumous collection of Steve Kowit's poems. We approached Mary, his wife, with our project and asked if she would like to help us. She agreed to assist us.

During the last year, I have spent my time reading and reflecting on Steve's poems. As the project developed discussing these poems with Jim made things move quickly. I look back at this time as an exciting exploration of a poet I respect not only as a writer but as a teacher.

In the end, I discovered that these poems demonstrate the clarity of Steve's perception as well as his love of nature and humanity. It was his love of the world that made him a poet and teacher. I was honored to study under him as well as be his friend.

Hasta proxima mi hermano,

— JOE MILOSCH

Steve Kowit: A Voice for the Voiceless

heard him read at an open mic in the early '90s. I was so amazed at the power of his poems, how he read, nodding his head, dipping his shoulders, looking up from his poem, looking at everyone in the room one at a time. It was as if he was reading to each of us. Like we were the best of friends.

I found out that he was a professor at Southwestern College so I went to see how he taught. And, oh man, how he taught! So, I kept going to his classes. Many classes over a thirty-year time period. He was a stickler for clarity, detail, and the magic of each person's memory. I carry him with me that way when I teach.

Steve was a fearless advocate for the Palestinians to have a homeland, and a voice for animals to have shelter and not be abused. Steve was a poet zealot against the difficult, esoteric poem, and an advocate for the poem/story. He effused these qualities when he read in public.

I miss him very much. I miss his voice in these times of amplified hate and ignorance.

Rest in Peace teacher/friend
Leah Kikich Wun

— JIM HORNSBY MORENO

ABOUT THE EDITORS

JOE MILOSCH was formally educated in the public schools and at San Diego State University.

His book, *Homeplate Was the Heart & Other Stories*, was nominated for the American Book Award, and he has multiple nominations for the Pushcart Prize in poetry. His other books are *Lost Pilgrimage Poems* and *Landscape of a Hummingbird*.

JIM HORNSBY MORENO is the author of *Dancing in Dissent: Poetry For Activism* (Dolphin Calling Press: 2007) and two CDs of poetry & music.

He is a Teaching Artist & on the Program Committee of San Diego Writers, Ink, and a Regional Editor of the *San Diego Poetry Annual.*

About the Artist

MARY KOWIT is a visual artist working in many forms of media. Most recently she has been doing jewelry making and copper enameling. She and Steve were together for 49 years after meeting while both working at the San Francisco Post Office. She now lives in rural East San Diego County near the Mexican border.

Acknowledgments

Some of these poems have appeared in *Antenna, California Quarterly, Caprice, Chiron Review, City Bender, Contact/11, Cover Arts New York, Exquisite Corpse, Friction, Hiram Poetry Review, Mangrove, Margie, Triplopia, Sun Magazine, The Spirit That Moves Us, The New York Quarterly, Titmouse Review, Vagabond, Willmore City, The Wormwood Review,* and *Yellow Silk.*

Some poems originally appeared in the following anthologies and books: *An Eye for an Eye Makes the Whole World Blind: Poets on 9/11, In the Palm of Your Hand, Orpheus and Company: Contemporary Poems on Greek Mythology,* and *The Poetry of Men's Lives: An International Anthology,* and the *San Diego Poetry Annual.*

Longer versions of the poem *Intifada* were previously published in a chapbook, titled *Intifada* in 2005 & 2015.

Credits

Cover:

> *Monoprint,* by MARY KOWIT

Section pages: Art by MARY KOWIT

Frog	3
Keys	15
Checkers	27
Laundromat	33
Worms	49
Monoprint	63
Birds & Border	77
Boat on Water	97
Penguins	103
Self Portrait	109
Big Rig	117
Truck Driver	123

Cover photographs: *(top to bottom)*

Smiling: photographer unknown (1996)
With Ford Econoline van, in Maryland, headed to Mexico: MARY KOWIT (1973)
Steve and Mary, with cats Frankie & Clementine: LIZ PETRANGELO (2007)
Visiting his boyhood home in Brooklyn: MARY KOWIT (1980)
Head shot for a visa in Mexico: FOTO GISMONDI (1973)
Necktie t-shirt: DIANE GAGE (1980)

Cover Design: RILEY PRATO

End Papers

About those three gents

Gents. Not old men, geezers, or duffers. Gents. Not old-fashioned gentlemen, but an echo of that. They're "elderly gents," all with an eye for the beauties of younger — and no longer attainable — females. These particular old gents are academics and love to discuss arcane subject matters, "matters subtle & abstruse, as is our wont."

It would not do the poet or poem justice for me (as one of the dedicatees) to make too much of any historical facts or context behind the poem, but a few might prove interesting. All through the last three decades of the 20th century and the first decade of the 21st, Steve, Fred and I hiked and walked many a mile through the Cuyamacas, Lagunas, and along San Diego's beaches. If only we'd recorded some of our conversations! Or, perhaps better we didn't. Yet, it would be fun to have a recording of one of our "scientific" conversations (three poets, mind you) on how seeing and hearing were forms of touching, after all, i.e., sound waves as air bumping against eardrums, light as "particles" entering the eye/brain. Ergo, touch! Maybe those cavorting 20-year-olds are not so unattainable after all.

Two habits on our hikes bear mentioning: we almost always brought drafts of poems we were working on to share and discuss during food breaks, and we almost always set aside 10 or 15 minutes to walk in silence, just paying attention to where our feet were landing, and enjoying trees, bird songs, or ocean waves. (We'd all been influenced by Zen and other meditative approaches.) It always seemed to me that after the silent walking our conversations quieted down and deepened somehow, and that we appreciated each other more and the time we were sharing together. That time, alas, now gone – though memorialized in poetry.

— AL ZOLYNAS

Fred Moramarco, Al Zolynas, Steve Kowit
Poseidon, Del Mar (2010)

128

About the poem, *Three Gents*

T*hree Gents* is a poem of eros, eros of body and mind, the love that imbues everything and usually can be approached only obliquely. The poet narrator takes delight in all of it. He feels the keen engagement of the discussion of ideas, paradoxes, dilemmas, the wonder of trying to decipher how the universe is put together. If only we could understand this, or that. If only we could take it apart and put it back together. And while we're doing that, the world in its ineffable beauty and mystery unfolds itself gorgeously, and unattainably. Do the three elder gents find solace in their endless discussion? Probably it affords them a measure of the illusion of control. Does it bring relief to the "carnal itch"? Probably not, but what are they to do now in their implacable aging? Talk. Debate. Wrangle. In the end, hopefully, laugh at themselves.

A villanelle, this poem exhibits the best of its kind as an exercise in trying to resolve obsessive thoughts. Thoughts that circle around some recurring topic, some something that seeks clarification. With villanelles, as with all good poems, paraphrases of content are far less than the sum of their parts: three old guys immersed in abstract discussions barely notice the world going by. No, that's not quite it. Three old guys debate and discuss abstruse topics as a guard against the unattainable beauty and impermanence of the world even as they move through it. Well, sort of.

This villanelle stands as a perfect example of what a good poem is, a mystery, a thing of delight, a something that has peered into the nature of things and given it to us such that we can do naught but look on in wonder.

— AL ZOLYNAS

The Three Gents: Steve, Fred, Al
Mary Kowit (1992)

Near and Far (Garden Oak Press: 2019) is the newest poetry collection by AL ZOLYNAS.

129

Also by Steve Kowit:

POETRY

Climbing the Walls
Cutting Our Loses
Heart in Utter Confusion
Lurid Confessions
Passionate Journey
Pranks
Mysteries of the Body
For My Birthday
Epic Journeys, Unbelievable Escapes
The Gods of Rapture
Crossing Borders
The First Noble Truth
The Dumbbell Nebula
Steve Kowit's Greatest Hits

ANTHOLOGIES

The Maverick Poets (editor)

TRANSLATION

Incitement to Nixonicide and Praise for the Chilean Revolution,
  Pablo Neruda

ON WRITING

In the Palm of Your Hand: The Poet's Portable Workshop

Among the elements

At Tor House (1984)

Steps going down, Esalen

**Lecturing the elements
The Cuyamacas** (2001)

At the beach

131

With visiting poet Jack Marshall
Naomi Schwartz

With Penny Perry
Taax, for *SDPA* (2012)

Steve introduces U.S. Poet Laureate Billy Collins at D.G. Wills bookstore.
Dennis Wills (2008)

Steve with featured poets at Coronado Library:
(l-r) Ron Salisbury, Una Nichols Hynum, Maria Mazziotti Gillan,
Seretta Martin, Mai-Lon Gittelsohn, Sharon Elise
Taax, for *SDPA* (2012)

132

with Abby
Mary Kowit (2009)

Steve attends a poetry reading
(2001)

Listening at Jewish Voice for
Peace, conference (2013)

At his home office
© Joan Gannij (1979)

At home
Mary Kowit (2010)

About Steve Kowit

S TEVE KOWIT grew up in Brooklyn, New York, and after a stint in the US Army Reserves moved to the West Coast. When the Vietnam War — what he called, "America's genocidal slaughter of the Vietnamese people" — began in earnest, he sent the Army a letter refusing to participate, and spent the next few years in Mexico and Central and South America. After the war ended, he settled in San Diego, where he founded that area's first animal rights organization.

He is the author of several collections of poetry and the recipient of a National Endowment Fellowship in Poetry, two Pushcart Prizes, a San Diego Book Award, the Theodor Seuss Geisel Award (2007), and other honors.

Steve taught at San Diego State University, San Diego City College, UC San Diego, and Southwestern College, and lived in the backcountry hills near the Tecate, Mexico, border with his beloved wife Mary and several animal companions.

He was the Poetry Editor, in Memoriam, of *Serving House: A Journal of Literary Arts.*

The Steve Kowit Poetry Prize, established in his honor in 2015, the year of his death, by the *San Diego Poetry Annual* and its sponsoring non-profit, the San Diego Entertainment + Arts Guild, presents a $1000 cash prize ($1350 in total cash awards), with poems by honorees published in the *SDPA* each March. The San Diego Public Library serves as the permanent home of The Kowit awards ceremony.

Enter Steve Kowit
Mary Kowit (1985)

134